Minna no Nihongo II

みんなの日本語

初級II 翻訳・文法解説 英語版
Translation & Grammatical Notes

スリーエーネットワーク

Published by 3A Corporation.
Shoei Bldg., 6-3, Sarugaku-cho 2-chome, Chiyoda-ku, Tokyo 101-0064, Japan

ISBN4-88319-108-7 C0081

First published 1998
Printed in Japan

FOREWORD

As the title **Minna no Nihongo** indicates, this book has been designed to make the study of Japanese as enjoyable and interesting as possible for students and teachers alike. Over three years in the planning and compilation, it stands as a complete textbook in itself while acting as a companion volume to the highly regarded **Shin Nihongo no Kiso.**

As readers may know, **Shin Nihongo no Kiso** is a comprehensive introduction to elementary Japanese that serves as a highly efficient resource enabling students wishing to master basic Japanese conversation to do so in the shortest possible time. As such, although it was originally developed for use by AOTS's technical trainees, it is now used by a wide range of people both in Japan and abroad.

The teaching of Japanese is branching out in many different ways. The growth in international relations has led to a greater level of interchange between Japan and other countries, and non-Japanese from a wide variety of backgrounds have come to Japan with a range of different objectives and are now living within local communities here. The changes in the social environment surrounding the teaching of Japanese that have resulted from this influx of people from other countries have in turn influenced the individual situations in which Japanese is taught. There is now a greater diversity of learning needs, and they require individual responses.

It is against this background, and in response to the opinions and hopes expressed by a large number of people who have been involved in the teaching of Japanese for many years both in Japan and elsewhere, that 3A Corporation proudly publishes **Minna no Nihongo**. While the book continues to make use of the clarity and ease of understanding provided by the special features, key learning points and learning methods of **Shin Nihongo no Kiso**, the scenes, situations and characters in **Minna no Nihongo** have been made more universal in order to appeal to a wider range of learners. Its contents have been enhanced in this way to allow all kinds of students to use it for studying Japanese with pleasure.

Minna no Nihongo is aimed at anyone who urgently needs to learn to communicate in Japanese in any situation, whether at work, school, college or in their local community. Although it is an introductory text, efforts have been made to make the exchanges between Japanese and foreign characters in the book reflect Japanese social conditions and everyday life as faithfully as possible. While it is intended principally for those who have already left full-time education, it can also be recommended as an excellent textbook for university entrance courses as well as short-term intensive courses at technical colleges and universities.

We at 3A Corporation are continuing actively to produce new study materials designed to meet the individual needs of an increasingly wide range of learners, and we sincerely hope that readers will continue to give us their valued support.

In conclusion, I should like to mention the extensive help we received in the preparation of this text, in the form of suggestions and comments from various quarters and trials of the materials in actual lessons, for which we are extremely grateful. 3A Corporation intends to continue extending its network of friendship all over the world through activities such as the publishing of Japanese study materials, and we hope that everyone who knows us will continue to lend us their unstinting encouragement and support in this.

3A Corporation

June 1998

EXPLANATORY NOTES

I. Structure

「みんなの日本語 初級II」consists of a Main Text, a Translation and Grammar Text and a set of cassette tapes/CDs. The Translation and Grammar Text is currently available in English. Versions in other languages will be published shortly. The materials have been prepared with the main emphasis on listening and speaking Japanese; they do not provide instruction in reading and writing hiragana, katakana or kanji.

II. Content and Method of Use

1. Main Text

1) Lessons

There are 25 lessons, from Lesson 26 to Lesson 50, which follow 「みんなの日本語 初級I」, and each contains the following:

① Sentence Patterns

Basic sentence patterns are shown.

② Example Sentences

A small dialogue in the style of a question and answer is given to show how the sentence patterns are used in practical conversation. New adverbs, conjunctions, and other grammatical points are also introduced.

③ Conversation

In the conversations, various foreign people staying in Japan appear in a variety of situations. The conversation includes everyday expressions and greetings. As they are simple, learning them by heart is recommended. If time allows, students should try developing the conversation by applying the reference words given in each lesson of the Translation and Grammar Text in order to maximize their communication skills.

④ Drills

The drills are divided into three levels: A, B, and C.

Drill A is visually designed in chart style to help understanding of the grammatical structure. The style helps students to learn systematically the basic sentence patterns through substitution drills, and applying verb forms and conjugations following the chart.

Drill B has various drill patterns to strengthen students' grasp of the basic sentence patterns. Follow the directions given in each practice. Drills marked with a ☞ sign use pictorial charts.

Drill C is given in discourse style to show how the sentence patterns function in actual situations, and to enhance practical oral skills. Do not simply read, repeat and substitute, but try making your own substitution, enrich the content, and develop the story.

⑤ Practice

Two kinds of practices are given: one type for listening (♮) and the other for grammar practice.

The listening practice is further divided into questions asking for personal answers, and questions confirming the key point of the given discourse. The listening practices are designed to strengthen students' aural skills, while the grammar practices check comprehension of vocabulary and the grammar points in the lessons studied.

The reading practices mostly require students to give a true or false response after reading a simple story compiled with words and sentence patterns from the lessons learned.

2) Review

This is provided to enable students to go over the essential points every several lessons studied.

3) Summary

At the end of the Main Text, a summary of grammatical points is given, such as the use of the particles, verb forms, adverbs and conjunctions, using example sentences appearing in the respective lessons.

4) Index

This includes classroom expressions, greetings, numerals, new vocabulary, and idiomatic expressions introduced in each lesson of the Main Text all through from Lesson 1 to Lesson 50.

2. Translation and Grammar Text

1) The following are given in each of the lessons from Lesson 26 to Lesson

50.

① new vocabulary and its translation

② translation of Sentence Patterns, Example Sentences, and Conversation

③ useful words related to the lesson and small pieces of information on Japan and the Japanese

④ explanation of essential grammar appearing in the lesson

2) A grammatical summary of particles, how to use the forms, adverbs, adverbial expressions, and various conjugations is given in English at the back of the Main Text.

3. Cassette Tapes/CDs

On the cassette tapes/CDs, Vocabulary, Sentence Patterns, Example Sentences, Drill C, Conversation and listening comprehension questions of the Practice section are recorded.

Students should pay attention to the pronunciation and intonation when listening to the Vocabulary, Sentence Patterns and Example Sentences. When listening to Drill C and Conversation, try to get accustomed to the natural speed of the language.

4. Kanji Usage

1) Kanji usage is based on 常用漢字表, which is an official list of the most commonly used Chinese characters in Japan.

① 熟字訓 (words which are made by a combination of two or more kanji and have a special reading) shown in the Appendix Chart of 常用漢字表 are written in kanji.

　　　e.g. 友達　friend　　果物　fruit　　眼鏡　glasses

② Proper nouns are written with their own Chinese characters even if their readings are non-standard.

　　　e.g. 大阪　Osaka　　奈良　Nara　　歌舞伎　Kabuki

2) For freeing students from confusion, some words are given in kana although they are included in 常用漢字表 and its Appendix Chart.

　　　e.g. ある（有る・在る）　　たぶん（多分）　　きのう（昨日）

　　　　　possess　exist　　　　perhaps　　　　yesterday

3) Numbers are principally shown in Arabic numerals.

e.g. 9 時 9 o'clock　　4 月 1 日　1st April　　1 つ　one (thing)

However kanji is used in the following cases.

e.g. 一人で　　　一度　　　　　一万円札

by oneself　　one time　　　ten thousand yen bill

5. Miscellaneous

1) Words which can be omitted from a sentence are enclosed in square brackets [ ].

e.g. 父は 54[歳] です。　　My father is 54 years old.

2) Synonyms are enclosed in round brackets (　).

e.g. だれ（どなた）　　who

3) The part for an alternative word is denoted by 〜.

e.g. 〜は いかがですか。　　How would you like 〜 ?

If the alternative part is a numeral, − is used.

e.g. −歳　−years old　　−円　−yen　　−時間　−hours

TO USERS OF THIS TEXTBOOK
The most effective way to study

1. Learn each word carefully.

The Translation & Grammatical Notes introduces the new words for each lesson. First, listen to the tape/CD and learn these words thoroughly, paying special attention to the correct pronunciation and accent. Try to make sentences with the new words. It is important to memorize not only a word itself, but its use in a sentence.

2. Practice the sentence patterns.

Make sure you understand the meaning of each sentence pattern, and do *Drills A* and *B* until you have mastered the pattern. Say the sentences aloud, especially when doing *Drill B*.

3. Practice the conversation drills.

Sentence-pattern practice is followed by conversation practice. The example conversations show the various situations in actual daily life in which people from abroad will often need to use Japanese. Start by doing *Drill C* to get accustomed to the pattern. Don't practice only the dialogue pattern, but try to expand the dialogue. And learn how to communicate suitably according to the situations by practicing the conversation.

4. Listen to the cassette tape/CD repeatedly.

When practicing *Drill C* and *Conversation*, listen to the tape/CD and say the dialogue aloud to make sure you acquire the correct pronunciation and intonation. Listening to the tape/CD is the most effective way to get used to the sound and speed of Japanese and to improve your listening ability.

5. Always remember to review and prepare.

So as not to forget what you have learnt in class, always review it the same day. Finally, do the practice section at the end of each lesson in order to check what you have learnt and to test your listening comprehension. As for the reading practice, this is an exercise to improve your comprehension of written material. Try to read it, referring to the vocabulary list. And, if you have time, look through the words and grammar explanation for the next lesson. Basic preparation is necessary for effective study.

6. Use what you have learnt.

Don't limit your learning to the classroom. Try to talk to Japanese people. Using what you have just learnt is the best way to progress.

If you complete this textbook following the above suggestions, you will have acquired the basic vocabulary and expressions necessary for daily life in Japan.

CHARACTERS IN THE CONVERSATIONS

Mike Miller
American, employee of IMC

Matsumoto Tadashi
Japanese, department
chief at IMC (Osaka)

Nakamura Akiko
Japanese, sales section
chief at IMC

Suzuki Yasuo
Japanese,
employee of IMC

Lee Jin Ju
Korean, researcher at AKC

Thawaphon
Thai, student at Sakura University

Ogawa Hiroshi
Japanese, neighbor
of Mike Miller's

Ogawa Yone
Japanese,
Ogawa Hiroshi's mother

Ogawa Sachiko
Japanese,
housewife

Karl Schmidt

German, engineer at Power Electric Company

Klara Schmidt

German, teacher of German

Watanabe Akemi

Japanese,
employee of
Power Electric Company

Takahashi Toru

Japanese,
employee of
Power Electric Company

Hayashi Makiko

Japanese,
employee of
Power Electric Company

John Watt

British, professor at
Sakura University

Ito Chiseko

Japanese, teacher in charge of
Hans Schmidt's class at
Himawari elementary school

Other Characters

Hans

German, schoolboy (12 yrs.),
son of Karl and Klara Schmidt

Gupta

Indian, employee of IMC

※IMC（computer software company）
※AKC（アジア研究センター：Asia Research Institute）

CONTENTS

Grammar Explanations and Reference Words & Information
in みんなの日本語 初級Ⅰ

Terms Used For Instruction

第一課	lesson -
文型	sentence pattern
例文	example sentence
会話	conversation
練習	practice
問題	exercise
答え	answer
読み物	reading practice
復習	review
目次	contents
索引	index
文法	grammar
文	sentence
単語（語）	word
句	phrase
節	clause
発音	pronunciation
母音	vowel
子音	consonant
拍	mora
アクセント	accent
イントネーション	intonation
[か]行	[か]-row
[い]列	[い]-line
丁寧体	polite style of speech
普通体	plain style of speech
活用	inflection
フォーム	form
〜形	〜 form
修飾	modification
例外	exception

名詞	noun
動詞	verb
自動詞	intransitive verb
他動詞	transitive verb
形容詞	adjective
い形容詞	い-adjective
な形容詞	な-adjective
助詞	particle
副詞	adverb
接続詞	conjunction
数詞	quantifier
助数詞	counter
疑問詞	interrogative (question word)
名詞文	noun (predicate) sentence
動詞文	verb (predicate) sentence
形容詞文	adjective (predicate) sentence
主語	subject
述語	predicate
目的語	object
主題	topic
肯定	affirmative
否定	negative
完了	perfective
未完了	imperfective
過去	past
非過去	non-past
可能	potential
意向	volitional
命令	imperative
禁止	prohibitive
条件	conditional
受身	passive
使役	causative
尊敬	respectful
謙譲	humble

Abbreviations

N   noun （名詞）

            e.g.   がくせい   つくえ
                   student   desk

い-adj   い-adjective （い形容詞）

            e.g.   おいしい   たかい
                   tasty   high

な-adj   な-adjective （な形容詞）

            e.g.   きれい[な]   しずか[な]
                   beautiful   quiet

V   verb （動詞）

            e.g.   かきます   たべます
                   write   eat

S   sentence （文）

            e.g.   これは 本です。
                This is a book.

                わたしは あした 東京へ 行きます。
                I will go to Tokyo tomorrow.

Lesson 26

I. Vocabulary

みます Ⅱ	見ます、診ます	check
さがします Ⅰ	探します、捜します _(thing)_	look for, search
おくれます Ⅱ [じかんに〜]	遅れます _(person)_ [時間に〜]	be late [for an appointment, etc.]
まに あいます Ⅰ [じかんに〜]	間に 合います [時間に〜]	be in time [for an appointment, etc.]
やります Ⅰ		do
さんかします Ⅲ [パーティーに〜]	参加します	attend [a party]
もうしこみます Ⅰ	申し込みます	apply for, enter for
つごうが いい	都合が いい	convenient (concerning time)
つごうが わるい	都合が 悪い	inconvenient (concerning time)
きぶんが いい	気分が いい	feel well
きぶんが わるい	気分が 悪い	feel ill
しんぶんしゃ	新聞社	newspaper publishing company, newspaper office
じゅうどう	柔道	judo
うんどうかい	運動会	athletic meeting
ばしょ	場所	place
ボランティア		volunteer
〜べん	〜弁	〜 dialect
こんど	今度	next time, another time
ずいぶん		pretty, very
ちょくせつ	直接	directly
いつでも		any time
どこでも		anywhere
だれでも		anybody
なんでも	何でも	anything
こんな 〜		〜 like this
そんな 〜		〜 like that (near the listener)
あんな 〜		〜 like that (far from both the speaker and the listener)

※NHK　　　　　　　　　　　　　　　Nippon Hoso Kyokai (broadcasting company)

※こどもの 日　　　　　　　　　　　Children's Day

※エドヤストア　　　　　　　　　　　fictitious store

◁会 話▷

片づきます [荷物が〜] Ⅰ　　　　　[boxes] be put in order

ごみ　　　　　　　　　　　　　　　garbage, trash, dust

出します [ごみを〜] Ⅰ　　　　　put out [the trash]

燃えます [ごみが〜] Ⅱ　　　　　[trash] burn

月・水・金　　　　　　　　　　　　Monday, Wednesday and Friday

置き場　　　　　　　　　　　　　　place where something is put

横　　　　　　　　　　　　　　　　side

瓶　　　　　　　　　　　　　　　　bottle

缶　　　　　　　　　　　　　　　　can

[お]湯　　　　　　　　　　　　　　hot water

ガス　　　　　　　　　　　　　　　gas

〜会社　　　　　　　　　　　　　　〜 company

連絡します Ⅲ　　　　　　　　　　contact

困ったなあ。　　　　　　　　　　　What shall I do?

┈┈ 読み物 ┈┈

電子メール　　　　　　　　　　　　electronic mail

宇宙　　　　　　　　　　　　　　　space, universe

怖い　　　　　　　　　　　　　　　be afraid of

宇宙船　　　　　　　　　　　　　　spaceship

別の　　　　　　　　　　　　　　　another

宇宙飛行士　　　　　　　　　　　　astronaut

※土井 隆雄　　　　　　　　　　　Japanese astronaut (1955-　)

II. Translation

Sentence Patterns

1. I am going on a trip from tomorrow.
2. I would like to learn ikebana (flower arrangement). Could you kindly introduce a good teacher to me?

Example Sentences

1. Ms. Watanabe, you sometimes speak Osaka dialect.
   Have you lived in Osaka?
   ···Yes, I lived in Osaka until I was fifteen.
2. The design of your shoes is interesting. Where did you buy them?
   ···I bought this pair at Edoya Store. They are Spanish.
3. Why were you late?
   ···Because the bus didn't come.
4. Are you going to participate in the Athletic Meeting?
   ···No, I won't. I don't like sports so much.
5. I've written a letter in Japanese. Could you please check it for me?
   ···Yes, of course.
6. I want to tour NHK. How can I do that?
   ···You just go and ask. You can tour there any time.

Conversation

Where do I put the trash?

Janitor: Mr. Miller, have you finished settling into your apartment?

Miller: Yes, I almost have.
Er, I want to throw some trash away. Where do I put it?

Janitor: Trash that can be burned should be put out on Monday, Wednesday, and Friday mornings.
The trash and garbage collection point is next to the parking lot.

Miller: What about bottles and cans?

Janitor: Bottles and cans should be put out on Saturdays.

Miller: I see. And there's no hot water.

Janitor: Get in touch with the gas company, and they will soon come and fix it.

Miller: Oh, what shall I do? I don't have a phone.
Sorry, but would you mind contacting them for me?

Janitor: No, certainly not.

Miller: That's very kind of you. Thank you.

III. Reference Words & Information

ごみの出し方　REFUSE DISPOSAL

In order to reduce and recycle refuse, household waste is sorted into types and collected on different days. The designated collection sites and collection days vary from area to area. The following is an example of the regulations.

ごみ収集日のお知らせ
Refuse Collection Day Information

可燃ごみ（燃えるごみ）
Combustible Refuse

紙くず	paper
生ごみ	garbage

収集日：月・水・金曜日
Collection days: Mon., Wed. & Fri.

不燃ごみ（燃えないごみ）
Non-combustible Refuse

ガラス製品	glass
プラスチック製品	plastics
金属製台所用品	metal kitchen utensils

収集日：木曜日
Thursday

粗大ごみ
Bulky Refuse

家具	scrap furniture
家庭電化製品	electrical appliances
自転車	bicycles

収集日：第3火曜日
the third Tuesday

資源ごみ
Recyclable Refuse

空き缶	cans
空きびん	bottles
古新聞	newspaper

収集日：第2、第4火曜日
the second and fourth Tuesday

IV. Grammar Explanation

1.

V	plain form	
い-adj	plain form	んです
な-adj	plain form ~だ→~な	
N	~だ→~な	

〜んです is an expression used to explain causes, reasons, grounds, etc., strongly. 〜んです is used in spoken language, while 〜のです is used in written language. 〜んです is used in the following ways.

1) | 〜んですか |

This expression is used in the following cases.

(1)When the speaker guesses the reason or the cause as to what he has seen or heard and then confirms whether he is correct.

① 渡辺さんは 時々 大阪弁を 使いますね。
　大阪に 住んで いたんですか。
　…ええ、15歳まで 大阪に 住んで いました。
　　Ms. Watanabe, you sometimes speak Osaka dialect.
　　Have you lived in Osaka?
　　…Yes, I lived in Osaka until I was fifteen.

(2)When the speaker asks for information about what he has seen or heard.

② おもしろい デザインの 靴ですね。どこで 買ったんですか。
　…エドヤストアで 買いました。
　　The design of your shoes is interesting. Where did you buy them?
　　…I bought this pair at Edoya Store.

(3)When the speaker asks the listener to explain the reason or the cause of what he has seen or heard.

③ どうして 遅れたんですか。
　　Why were you late?

(4)When asking for an explanation of a situation.

④ どう したんですか。
　　What's the matter?

[Note] "〜んですか" sometimes contains the speaker's surprise, suspicion, strong curiosity, etc. Inappropriate use, therefore, may offend the listener, so it is necessary to be careful with this expression.

2) | 〜んです |

This expression is used in the following cases.

(1)When stating the reason or cause as an answer to such questions as in (3) and (4) in 1) above.

⑤ どうして 遅れたんですか。　　　　　Why were you late?
　…バスが 来なかったんです。　　　　…Because the bus didn't come.

⑥ どう したんですか。　　　　　　　　What's the matter?
　…ちょっと 気分が 悪いんです。　　…I don't feel well.

(2)When the speaker adds the reason or the cause to what he's stated.

⑦ 毎朝 新聞を 読みますか。　　　Do you read a newspaper every morning?

　…いいえ。時間が ないんです。　　…No. I don't have the time.

[Note] ～んです is not used to merely describe the facts as shown in the following example.

　　わたしは マイク・ミラーです。　　I am Mike Miller.

　× わたしは マイク・ミラーなんです。

3) | ～んですが、～ |

～んですが is used to introduce a topic. It is followed by a request, an invitation or an expression seeking permission. が in this case is used to connect sentences lightly and indicates hesitation and reservation on the speaker's side. As in ⑩, clauses following ～んですが are often omitted when they are self-evident to the speaker and the listener.

⑧ 日本語で 手紙を 書いたんですが、ちょっと 見て いただけませんか。

　I've written a letter in Japanese. Could you please check it for me?

⑨ NHKを 見学したいんですが、どう したら いいですか。

　I want to tour NHK. How can I do that?

⑩ お湯が 出ないんですが……。

　There's no hot water.

2. | V て-form いただけませんか | 　Would you please do me the favor of ～ing?

This is a request expression that is politer than ～て ください。

⑪ いい 先生を 紹介して いただけませんか。

　Would you please introduce a good teacher to me?

✕ 3. | Interrogative V た-form ら いいですか | What/When/Where／Which/How/Who } shall I ～?　　*ask advice*

⑫ どこで カメラを 買ったら いいですか。　Where should I buy a camera?

⑬ 細かい お金が ないんですが、どう したら いいですか。

　I don't have any small change. What shall I do?

～たら いいですか is used when the speaker asks the listener for some advice or instructions about what to do. In ⑫, the speaker wants to buy a camera but does not know where to buy one, so he asks the listener to recommend a good shop.

4. | N (object)は { 好きです／嫌いです 　 上手です／下手です 　 あります, etc. } | like/dislike 　be good at/be poor at 　have, etc. } N |

⑭ 運動会に 参加しますか。

　…いいえ。スポーツは あまり 好きじゃ ないんです。

　Are you going to participate in the athletic meeting?

　…No. I don't like sports very much.

You learned in Book Ⅰ (Lessons 10 and 17) that subjects and also objects indicated by を can become topics and be highlighted by は. Objects indicated by が can also be highlighted by は.

Lesson 27

I.   Vocabulary

かいます Ⅰ	飼います	keep (a pet), raise (an animal)
たてます Ⅱ	建てます	build
はしります Ⅰ	走ります	run, drive [along a road]
[みちを～]	[道を～]	
とります Ⅰ	取ります	take [a holiday]
[やすみを～]	[休みを～]	
みえます Ⅱ	見えます	[a mountain] can be seen
[やまが～]	[山が～]	
きこえます Ⅱ	聞こえます	[a sound] can be heard
[おとが～]	[音が～]	
できます Ⅱ		[an airport] be made, be completed, come into
[くうこうが～]	[空港が～]	existence
ひらきます Ⅰ	開きます	set up [a class], open, hold
[きょうしつを～]	[教室を～]	
ペット		pet
とり	鳥	bird
こえ	声	voice
なみ	波	wave
はなび	花火	fireworks
けしき	景色	scenery, view
ひるま	昼間	daytime
むかし	昔	old days, ancient times
どうぐ	道具	tool, instrument, equipment
じどうはんばいき	自動販売機	vending machine
つうしんはんばい	通信販売	mail order, mail-order sales
クリーニング		(dry) cleaning, laundry
マンション		condominium, apartment house
だいどころ	台所	kitchen
～きょうしつ	～教室	～ class
パーティールーム		party room
～ご	～後	after ～ (duration of time)
～しか		only ～ (used with negatives)
ほかの		other

はっきり	clearly
ほとんど	almost all (in affirmative sentences), hardly, scarcely (in negative sentences)
※関西空港	Kansai International Airport
※秋葉原	name of a shopping district in Tokyo with many electrical stores
※伊豆	peninsula in Shizuoka Prefecture

◀ 会 話 ▶

日曜大工	Sunday carpenter
本棚	bookshelf
夢	dream (〜を みます: have a dream)
いつか	someday, sometime
家	house, home
すばらしい	marvelous, wonderful

····· 読み物 ·····

子どもたち	children
大好き［な］	like very much
漫画	cartoon, comic strip
主人公	hero, heroine
形	shape
ロボット	robot
不思議［な］	fantastic, mysterious
ポケット	pocket
例えば	for example
付けます Ⅱ	attach, put on
自由に	freely
空	sky
飛びます Ⅰ	fly
自分	oneself
将来	future
※ドラえもん	name of a cartoon character

II. Translation

Sentence Patterns

1. I can speak Japanese a little.
2. We can see a town from the top of the mountain.
3. They have built a big supermarket in front of the station.

Example Sentences

1. Can you read Japanese newspapers?
   ⋯No, I can't.
2. How many days summer vacation can you take at Power Electric?
   ⋯Well, about three weeks.
   That's good. I can take only one week at my company.
3. Can you keep pets in this condominium?
   ⋯We can keep a little bird or fish, but not a dog or a cat.
4. Can you see Mt. Fuji from Tokyo?
   ⋯In the old days we could see it well, but now we can hardly see it at all.
5. You can hear birds singing, can't you?
   ⋯Yes. Spring has come.
6. When did they complete Kansai International Airport?
   ⋯In the autumn of 1994.
7. That's a nice bag. Where did you buy it?
   ⋯I bought it by mail order.
   Do they also have it in department stores?
   ⋯I think they don't have it in department stores.

Conversation

You can make anything, can't you?

Suzuki: What with all the light it gets, it's a nice room.
Miller: Yes. You can see the ocean on a fine day.
Suzuki: This table has an interesting design, doesn't it?
         Did you buy it in the States?
Miller: No, I made it myself.
Suzuki: Oh, really?
Miller: Yes. Do-it-yourself is my hobby.
Suzuki: Wow. Did you make that bookshelf, too?
Miller: Yes.
Suzuki: That's amazing! You can make anything, can't you?
Miller: It's my dream to build my own house by myself someday.
Suzuki: That's a wonderful dream.

III. Reference Words & Information

近くの店　SHOPS FOUND LOCALLY

写真屋　Camera Shop

現像	developing
プリント	printing
焼き増し	extra print
引き伸ばし	enlargement
ネガ	negative
スライド	slide
サービスサイズ	service size
パノラマサイズ	panoramic size

クリーニング屋　Cleaners

ドライクリーニング	dry cleaning
水洗い	laundering
染み抜き	stain removal
防水加工	waterproof
サイズ直し	alterations
縮む	shrink
伸びる	stretch

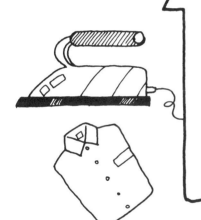

コンビニ　Convenience Store

宅配便の受付	delivery service
写真現像	photo developing
公共料金振り込み	payment of utility charges
コピー、ファクス	photocopy, fax
はがき、切手の販売	sale of postcards and stamps
コンサートチケットの販売	sale of concert tickets

IV. Grammar Explanation

1. Potential verbs ("can")

How to make potential verbs (See Main Textbook, Lesson 27, p.12, 練習 A1.)

		Potential verbs	
		polite form	plain form
I	かきます	かけます	かける
	かいます	かえます	かえる
II	たべます	たべられます	たべられる
III	きます	こられます	こられる
	します	できます	できる

All potential verbs are Group II verbs; they conjugate into the dictionary form, ない-form, て-form, etc.

 e.g. かける, かけ(ない), かけて

わかる, which includes the meaning of possibility itself, does not change into わかれる.

2. Potential verb sentences

1) Potential verbs express not actions but states. The objects of transitive verbs are indicated by the particle を. When they become potential verbs, however, their objects are usually indicated by the particle が.

 ① わたしは 日本語を 話します。 I speak Japanese.
 ② わたしは 日本語が 話せます。 I can speak Japanese.

No particles change except for を.

 ③ 一人で 病院へ 行けますか。 Can you go to the hospital alone?
 ④ 田中さんに 会えませんでした。 I could not see Mr. Tanaka.

2) Potential verbs have two uses: to express a person's ability to do something (⑤) and to express the possibility of an action in a certain situation (⑥).

 ⑤ ミラーさんは 漢字が 読めます。 Mr. Miller can read kanji.
 ⑥ この 銀行で ドルが 換えられます。 You can change dollars at this bank.

3. 見えます and 聞こえます

The potential verb for みます is みられます and that for ききます is きけます. They indicate that one's intention of seeing or listening can be realized. みえます indicates that a certain object comes into one's sight and きこえます that a sound reaches one's ears independent of one's will. In sentences using みえます and きこえます, objects to be seen or heard become the subjects of the sentence and are indicated by が.

 ⑦ 新宿で 今 黒沢の 映画が 見られます。
 You can now see Kurosawa's movies in Shinjuku.
 ⑧ 新幹線から 富士山が 見えます。
 Mt. Fuji can be seen from the Shinkansen.
 ⑨ 電話で 天気予報が 聞けます。
 You can hear the weather forecast by phone.
 ⑩ ラジオの 音が 聞こえます。
 The sound of a radio can be heard.

4．できます

The verb できます that you learn here means "come into being," "come up," "be completed," "be finished," "be made," etc.

⑪ 駅の 前に 大きい スーパーが できました。

A big supermarket has been completed in front of the station.

⑫ 時計の 修理は いつ できますか。

When can you fix this watch?

5．は

1) では／には／へは／からは／までは，etc.

は is used to highlight a noun as a topic, and as you learned in Lessons 10, 17 and 26, when が or を follows the noun, it is replaced by は. When other particles (e.g. で, に, へ, etc.) follow the noun, は is placed after them.

⑬ わたしの 学校には アメリカ人の 先生が います。

In my school there is an American teacher.

⑭ わたしの 学校では 中国語が 習えます。

In my school we can learn the Chinese language.

2) は used to make contrasts

⑮ きのうは 山が 見えましたが、きょうは 見えません。

Yesterday we could see mountains, but not today.

⑯ ワインは 飲みますが、ビールは 飲みません。

I drink wine, but not beer.

⑰ 京都へは 行きますが、大阪へは 行きません。

I will go to Kyoto, but not to Osaka.

6．も

Like the usage of は explained above, も replaces を or が, but follows other particles. In the case of the particle へ, however, it can be omitted.

⑱ クララさんは 英語が 話せます。フランス語も 話せます。

Klara can speak English. She can speak French, too.

⑲ 去年 アメリカへ 行きました。メキシコ［へ］も 行きました。

I went to America last year. I went to Mexico, too.

⑳ わたしの 部屋から 海が 見えます。弟の 部屋からも 見えます。

The sea can be seen from my room, and also from my brother's room.

7．しか

しか is attached to nouns, quantifiers, etc., and is always used with negative predicates. It highlights the word, makes limitations and negates everything except the thing expressed by the word. It replaces が or を, but follows other particles. しか has a negative nuance, while だけ has a positive one.

㉑ ローマ字しか 書けません。

I cannot write anything but Roman letters.

㉒ ローマ字だけ 書けます。

I can only write Roman letters.

Lesson 28

I. Vocabulary

うれます Ⅱ 　[パンが〜]	売れます	[bread] sell, be sold
おどります I	踊ります	dance
かみます I		chew, bite
えらびます I	選びます	choose
ちがいます I	違います	be different
かよいます I 　[だいがくに〜]	通います 　[大学に〜]	go to and from [university]
メモします Ⅲ		take a memo
まじめ[な]		serious
ねっしん[な]	熱心[な]	earnest
やさしい	優しい	gentle, kind
えらい	偉い	great, admirable
ちょうど いい		proper, just right
しゅうかん	習慣	custom
けいけん	経験	experience
ちから	力	power
にんき	人気	popularity ([がくせいに] 〜が あります: be popular [with students])
かたち	形	form, shape
いろ	色	color
あじ	味	taste
ガム		chewing gum
しなもの	品物	goods
ねだん	値段	price
きゅうりょう	給料	salary
ボーナス		bonus
ばんぐみ	番組	program
ドラマ		drama
しょうせつ	小説	novel

しょうせつか	小説家	novelist
かしゅ	歌手	singer
かんりにん	管理人	janitor
むすこ	息子	(my) son
むすこさん	息子さん	(someone else's) son
むすめ	娘	(my) daughter
むすめさん	娘さん	(someone else's) daughter
じぶん	自分	oneself
しょうらい	将来	future
しばらく		a little while
たいてい		usually, mostly
それに		in addition
それで		and so

◀会話▶

[ちょっと] お願いが あるんですが。	I have a favor to ask.
ホームステイ	homestay
会話	conversation
おしゃべりします Ⅲ	chat

------ 読み物 ------

お知らせ	notice
日にち	date
土	Saturday
体育館	gymnasium
無料	free of charge

II. Translation

Sentence Patterns

1. I listen to music while eating.
2. I jog every morning.
3. Subways are fast and inexpensive, so let's take the subway.

Example Sentences

1. When I'm driving and sleepy, I chew gum.
   ···You do? I stop the car, and take a nap for a while.
2. Taro, don't watch TV while studying.
   ···OK, Mum.
3. He is working while studying at university.
   ···Really? He is admirable.
4. What do you usually do on holidays?
   ···Well, mostly I draw pictures.
5. Professor Watt is earnest, diligent and rich in experience.
   ···He is a good teacher, isn't he?
6. Mr. Tanaka, you often go on trips, but never go abroad.
   ···That's right. I don't understand foreign languages, and the customs are different from ours, and so travelling abroad is tough for me.

7. Why did you choose Sakura University?
   ···Sakura University is the one which my father graduated from, it has many good professors, and it is near to my house.

Conversation

Over a cup of tea

Ogawa Sachiko:	Mr. Miller, I have a favor to ask.
Miller:	What is it?
Ogawa Sachiko:	Would you mind teaching English to my son?
	He is going to Australia on a homestay program this summer vacation, but he can't speak English.
Miller:	I wish I could, but I'm afraid I don't have time to....
Ogawa Sachiko:	Couldn't you have a chat with him over a cup of tea?
Miller:	Well, I often have to go on business trips, and I'll soon have a Japanese language test....
	Besides I have never taught before....
Ogawa Sachiko:	So, you can't.... Well, that's a shame.
Miller:	I am very sorry.

III. Reference Words & Information

うちを借(か)りる　RENTING ACCOMMODATION

How to Read Housing Information

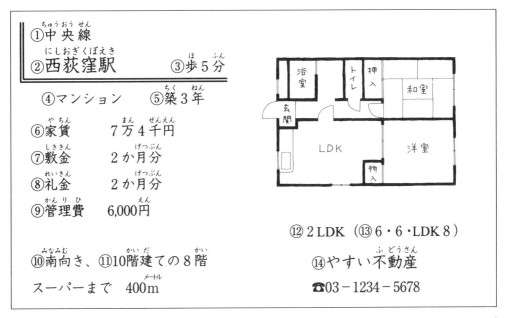

① train line
② nearest station
③ five-minute walk from the station
④ condominium made of reinforced concrete

　　※アパート　　　　　one or two-story wooden apartment building
　　　一戸建(いっこだ)て　　　　detached house, single house

⑤ three years old (years since construction)
⑥ rental fee
⑦ deposit money
　　※Money that's left with the owner in the form of a deposit.
　　　When you move out, the owner in principle gives a part of it back.
⑧ gift money
　　※Money that's paid directly to the owner as a "gift."
⑨ maintenance fee
⑩ facing south
⑪ 8th floor of ten-story building
⑫ living/dining room with kitchen and 2 rooms
⑬ 6 mats （＝ 6 畳(じょう)）
　　※'畳(じょう)' is a unit of measurement used for the area of a room.
　　　1畳(じょう) corresponds to the area of a tatami mat (approximately 180 × 90cm).
⑭ real estate agent

IV. Grammar Explanation

1. | V₁ ます-form ながら V₂ |

This sentence pattern means that one person does two different actions (V₁ and V₂) at the same time. The action denoted by V₂ is the more emphasized of the two actions.

① 音楽を 聞きながら 食事します。　　I listen to music while eating.

This sentence pattern is also used when the two actions take place over a period of time.

② 働きながら 日本語を 勉強して います。

I'm working and studying Japanese.

2. | Vて-form います |

An individual's customary action is expressed by this sentence pattern. A customary action in the past is expressed by using Vて-form いました.

③ 毎朝 ジョギングを して います。

I jog every morning.

④ 子どもの とき、毎晩 8時に 寝て いました。

I used to go to bed at eight every evening when I was a child.

3. | plain form し、～ |

1) When sentences are stated from a certain viewpoint, they can be linked using this structure. For example, sentences describing the merits of a particular subject are joined into one sentence using this pattern.

⑤ ワット先生は 熱心だし、まじめだし、経験も あります。

Professor Watt is earnest and diligent and has experience.

2) This structure is also used to state causes or reasons when there is more than one cause or reason. Use of this structure implies the meaning of "furthermore" or "on top of that."

⑥ 駅から 近いし、車でも 来られるし、この 店は とても 便利です。

This shop is very convenient. It's near the station, and you can also come here by car. When the speaker states reasons using this pattern, he/she sometimes does not say his/her conclusion when it's understood from the context. See ⑦.

⑦ 息子に 英語を 教えて いただけませんか。

…うーん、出張も 多いし、もうすぐ 日本語の 試験も あるし……。

Could you teach English to my son?

…Sorry. I often go on business trips, and I have to take a Japanese exam soon.

There are cases when only one ～し is used in a sentence. Though the reason explicitly stated is only one, the existence of other reasons is implied by the use of ～し. Note this is not true of ～から.

⑧ 色も きれいだし、この 靴を 買います。

Because the color is beautiful (and for some other reasons), I'll buy this pair of shoes.
As you see in ⑤, ⑥, ⑦ and ⑧, the particle も is often used in this sentence pattern. By the use of も, the speaker implies the existence of other reasons to emphasize his/her viewpoint.

4. それに

それに is used when you add another similar fact or situation.

⑨ どうして さくら大学を 選んだんですか。

…さくら大学は、父が 出た 大学だし、いい 先生も 多いし、それに 家から 近いですから。

Why did you choose Sakura University?

…Because it's my father's alma mater, there are many good teachers, and besides, it's near my house.

5. それで

それで is a conjunction used to show that what was said before it is the reason or cause for the sentence following it.

⑩ この レストランは 値段も 安いし、おいしいんです。

…それで 人が 多いんですね。

The food is inexpensive and tasty in this restaurant.

…And that's why it's crowded.

6. よく この 喫茶店に 来るんですか

In this sentence (see 練習 C 2), the particle に, which indicates one's destination, is used instead of the particle へ, which shows direction. Verbs like いきます, きます, かえります and しゅっちょうします are used with either "place へ" or "place に."

Lesson 29

I.　Vocabulary

あきます　I ［ドアが～］	開きます	[a door] open
しまります　I ［ドアが～］	閉まります	[a door] close, shut
つきます　I ［でんきが～］	［電気が～］	[a light] come on
きえます　II ［でんきが～］	消えます ［電気が～］	[a light] go off, disappear
こみます　I ［みちが～］	込みます ［道が～］	[a road] get crowded
すきます　I ［みちが～］	［道が～］	[a road] get empty
こわれます　II ［いすが～］	壊れます	[a chair] break
われます　II ［コップが～］	割れます	[a glass] break, smash
おれます　II ［きが～］	折れます ［木が～］	[a tree] break, snap
やぶれます　II ［かみが～］	破れます ［紙が～］	[the paper] tear
よごれます　II ［ふくが～］	汚れます ［服が～］	[the clothes] get dirty
つきます　I ［ポケットが～］	付きます	[a pocket] be attached
はずれます　II ［ボタンが～］	外れます	[a button] be undone
とまります　I ［エレベーターが～］	止まります	[an elevator] stop
まちがえます　II		make a mistake
おとします　I	落とします	drop, lose
かかります　I ［かぎが～］	掛かります	be locked
［お］さら	［お］皿	plate, dish
［お］ちゃわん		rice bowl
コップ		glass (vessel)

ガラス		glass (material)
ふくろ	袋	bag
さいふ	財布	wallet, purse
えだ	枝	branch, twig
えきいん	駅員	station employee
この へん	この 辺	this neighborhood, around here
～ へん	～ 辺	the place around ～
このくらい		about this size

おさきに どうぞ。	お先に どうぞ。	After you./Go ahead, please.
[ああ、] よかった。		Thank goodness! (used to express a feeling of relief)

◀会話▶

今の 電車	the train which has just left
忘れ物	things left behind, lost property
～側	～ side
ポケット	pocket
覚えて いません。	I don't remember.
網棚	rack
確か	I suppose, if I am correct
※四ツ谷	name of a station in Tokyo

····· 読み物 ·····

地震	earthquake
壁	wall
針	hands (of a clock)
指します I	point
駅前	the area in front of a station
倒れます II	fall down
西	west
方	direction
※三宮	name of a place in Kobe

II. Translation

Sentence Patterns

1. The window is closed.
2. This vending machine is broken.
3. I left my umbrella in a train.

Example Sentences

1. The door of the meeting room is locked.
   ···Then, let's ask Ms. Watanabe to unlock it.
2. May I use this fax?
   ···It's broken. So please use the one over there.
3. Where is the wine Mr. Schmidt brought?
   ···I'm afraid we drank it all.
4. Won't you go to eat lunch?
   ···I'm sorry, but I want to finish this letter. So, go ahead, please.
5. Were you in time for the Shinkansen?
   ···No. The road was crowded, so unluckily I was late.
6. I have lost my ticket. What shall I do?
   ···Tell the station employee over there, please.

Conversation

I left something

Lee:	Excuse me. I left something in the train that's just gone.
Station employee:	What did you leave?
Lee:	A blue bag. About this size.
	And it has a big pocket on the outside.
Employee:	Whereabouts did you leave it?
Lee:	I don't remember exactly. I put it on the rack.
Employee:	What's inside it?
Lee:	Let me think... books and an umbrella, if I remember right.
Employee:	Well, I'll ring up and check right away. Could you wait a moment, please?

Employee:	It's been found.
Lee:	Oh, what a relief!
Employee:	It's at Yotsuya Station. What do you want to do?
Lee:	I'll go and get it myself right away.
Employee:	Then, please go to the Yotsuya Station office.
Lee:	OK. Thank you very much.

III. Reference Words & Information

状態・様子　STATE & APPEARANCE

太っている　fat

やせている　thin

膨らんでいる
bulging

穴が開いている
have a hole

曲がっている　bent
umbrella

ゆがんでいる
distorted
(~face)

へこんでいる
dented

ねじれている
twisted
(belt, hair)

欠けている　chipped

ひびが入っている
cracked

腐っている　rotten

乾いている　dry

ぬれている　wet

凍っている　frozen

IV. Grammar Explanation

1. ┃ Ｖて-form います ┃

Ｖて-form います expresses the state which results as a consequence of the action expressed by the verb.

1) ┃ Ｎが Ｖて-form います ┃

① 窓が 割れて います。　　　　The window is broken.
② 電気が ついて います。　　　The light is on.

As in the examples above, when the speaker describes the state he/she sees in front of him/her as it is, the subject of the action is indicated with が. Example ① shows that "the window was broken in the past and at present its consequence remains (=it is broken)." Verbs which are used with this expression are intransitive verbs, and most of them indicate an instantaneous act or action. Examples of such verbs include こわれます, きえます, あきます, こみます, etc.

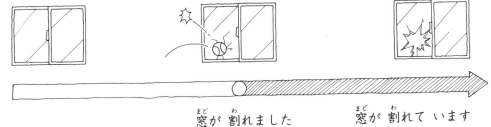

窓が 割れました　　　　　窓が 割れて います

When describing states in the past, Ｖて-form いました is used.

③ けさは 道が 込んで いました。　　The road was crowded this morning.

2) ┃ Ｎは Ｖて-form います ┃

When the subject of an act or action is taken up as a topic, it is indicated with は. In example ④, with the use of a demonstrative, この, the speaker clearly identifies the chair as the topic and describes the state of it to the listener.

④ この いすは 壊れて います。　　This chair is broken.

2. ┃ Ｖて-form しまいました／しまいます ┃

Ｖて-form しまいました is an expression which emphasizes that an action or event has been completed.

⑤ シュミットさんが 持って 来た ワインは 全部 飲んで しまいました。
We drank all the wine that Mr. Schmidt brought.

⑥ 漢字の 宿題は もう やって しまいました。
I have done my kanji homework already.

Though Ｖました can also indicate the completion of an action, the use of Ｖて-form しまいました emphasizes the actual completing of the action. Therefore, the latter is often accompanied by such adverbs as もう and/or ぜんぶ. Because of this feature of the expression, example ⑤ implies the resultant state, i.e., there is no wine left, and example ⑥ that the speaker's state of mind is one of relief.

Also, Ｖて-form しまいます expresses that the speaker will complete an action in the future.

⑦ 昼ごはんまでに レポートを 書いて しまいます。
   I intend to finish writing the report by lunch time.

3. | Ｖて-form しまいました |

This expression conveys the speaker's embarrassment or regret in a difficult situation.

⑧ パスポートを なくして しまいました。   I lost my passport.
⑨ パソコンが 故障して しまいました。   My personal computer's broken.

Though the fact of losing one's passport or the trouble with the computer can be expressed with なくしました or こしょうしました, these sentences above add the speaker's feeling of regret or embarrassment about the fact.

4. ありました

⑩ ［かばんが］ ありましたよ。   I've found [the bag].

ありました here is used to indicate that the speaker has found the bag, not to indicate that it existed some place in the past.

5. どこかで／どこかに

In the examples shown in Lesson 13, you learned へ in どこかへ and を in なにかを could be omitted. However, で in どこかで (⑪) or に in どこかに (⑫) cannot be omitted.

⑪ どこかで 財布を なくして しまいました。
   I've lost my wallet somewhere.
⑫ どこかに 電話が ありませんか。
   Is there a pay phone somewhere nearby?

29

27

Lesson 30

I. Vocabulary

はります I		* put up, post, paste
かけます II	掛けます	· hang
かざります I	飾ります	display, decorate
ならべます II	並べます	arrange, line up
うえます II	植えます	plant
もどします I	戻します	return, put 〜 back
まとめます II		put 〜 together, put 〜 in shape, sum up
かたづけます II	片づけます	put things in order, tidy up
しまいます I		put things in their proper place
きめます II	決めます	decide
しらせます II	知らせます	inform
そうだんします III	相談します	consult, discuss
よしゅうします III	予習します	prepare one's lesson
ふくしゅうします III	復習します	review one's lesson
そのままに します III		leave things as they are
おこさん	お子さん	(someone else's) child
じゅぎょう	授業	class
こうぎ	講義	lecture
ミーティング		meeting
よてい	予定	plan, schedule
おしらせ	お知らせ	notice
あんないしょ	案内書	guide book
カレンダー		calendar
ポスター		poster
ごみばこ	ごみ箱	trash can, dustbin
にんぎょう	人形	doll
かびん	花瓶	vase
かがみ	鏡	mirror
ひきだし	引き出し	drawer
げんかん	玄関	front door, porch, entrance hall
ろうか	廊下	corridor, hallway
かべ	壁	wall

いけ	池	pond
こうばん	交番	police box
もとの ところ	元の 所	original place
まわり	周り	round, around
まんなか	真ん中	center
すみ	隅	corner
まだ		still
～ほど		about ～

◁会話▷

予定表	schedule
ご苦労さま。	Thank you for your hard work. (used by a superior or older person to express appreciation for a subordinate's work)
希望	hope, request
何か ご希望が ありますか。	Do you have any requests?
ミュージカル	musical
それは いいですね。	That's a good idea./That sounds nice.
※ブロードウェイ	Broadway

····· 読み物 ·····

丸い	round
月	moon
ある ～	one ～, a certain ～
地球	earth
うれしい	glad, happy
嫌[な]	hateful, disagreeable
すると	and, then
目が 覚めます Ⅱ	wake up

II. Translation

Sentence Patterns

1. There is a map of the town affixed to the wall in the police box.
2. I will read a guide book before going on the trip.

Example Sentences

1. The new rest room in the station is interesting.
   ···Really?
   It has flowers and animals painted on the wall.
2. Where is the adhesive tape?
   ···It's kept in that drawer.
3. Have you already decided the name of your baby?
   ···No. I will think about it after I see its face.
4. What should I do before the next meeting?
   ···Read this data.
5. I would like to participate in volunteer activities, and so may I take leave for about two weeks?
   ···Two weeks? Let me see. I'll have to talk with the department manager about it.
6. When you finish using the scissors, return them to their original place.
   ···Yes, all right.

7. May I put this material away?
   ···No, leave it there.
      I'm still using it.

Conversation

I will reserve a ticket for you

Miller:	Ms. Nakamura, I have fixed the schedule and data for your trip to New York.
Nakamura:	Thank you. I will check the data later, so leave it there.
Miller:	Yes.
Nakamura:	Is this the schedule?
	Have you already contacted Mr. White?
Miller:	Yes.
	You are free on the afternoon of this day.
Nakamura:	Oh, I am.
Miller:	Is there something you want to do that day?
Nakamura:	Well, I think I'd like to see a musical on Broadway.
Miller:	That sounds nice. Shall I reserve a ticket for you?
Nakamura:	Yes, please.

III. Reference Words & Information

位置　LOCATION

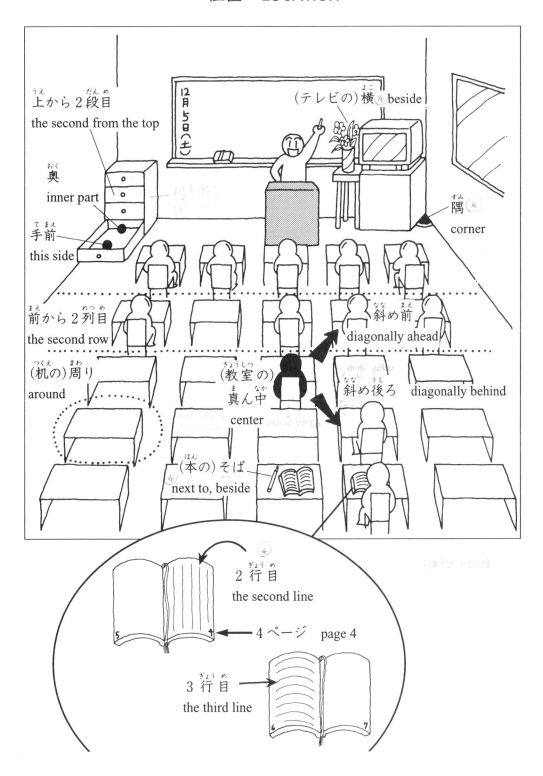

IV. Grammar Explanation

1. ┃ Ｖて-form あります ┃

Ｖて-form あります indicates the state which results as a consequence of an action intentionally done by somebody. The verbs used here are transitive verbs that express intentions.

1) ┃ N₁に N₂が Ｖて-form あります ┃

① 机の 上に メモが 置いて あります。　　　　There is a memo put on the desk.
② カレンダーに 今月の 予定が 書いて あります。
　　This month's schedule is written on the calendar.

In ①, it is indicated that someone put a memo on the desk (for later use) and as a result the memo exists as it was put. ② indicates that someone wrote this month's schedule on the calendar (so as not to forget it) and as a result the schedule is written on the calendar.

2) ┃ N₂は N₁に Ｖて-form あります ┃

This sentence pattern is used when N₂ in sentence pattern 1) is taken up as a topic.

③ メモは どこですか。　　　　　　　　　Where is the memo?
　　…［メモは］机の 上に 置いて あります。　…It's been put on the desk.
④ 今月の 予定は カレンダーに 書いて あります。
　　This month's schedule has been written on the calendar.

3) Ｖて-form あります is used to express the state of the result of what somebody did for some purpose. So it can also express, as in ⑤ and ⑥, that some preparation has been done. It is often used with もう.

⑤ 誕生日の プレゼントは もう 買って あります。
　　I have already bought the present for her birthday.
⑥ ホテルは もう 予約して あります。
　　I have already reserved a hotel.

[Note]　The difference between Ｖて-form います and Ｖて-form あります

⑦ 窓が 閉まって います。　　　　The window is closed.
⑧ 窓が 閉めて あります。　　　　The window has been closed (for some purpose).

⑦ simply describes the state that the window is closed, while ⑧ implies that somebody (it could be the speaker himself) closed the window with some objective or intention in mind. Most verbs used in Ｖて-form います are intransitive, while verbs used in Ｖて-form あります are transitive.

A lot of intransitive verbs have transitive counterparts and each pair shares a part in common. See Main Textbook, p. 228, 自動詞と他動詞.

2. ┃ Ｖて-form おきます ┃

This sentence pattern means:

1) Completion of a necessary action by a given time

⑨ 旅行の まえに 切符を 買って おきます。

I'll buy a ticket before the trip.

⑩ 次の 会議までに 何を して おいたら いいですか。

…この 資料を 読んで おいて ください。

What should I do before the next meeting?

…Read these materials.

2) Completion of a necessary action in readiness for the next use or the next step

⑪ はさみを 使ったら、元の 所に 戻して おいて ください。

When you finish using the scissors, put them back where they were.

3) Keeping the resultant state as it is

⑫ あした 会議が ありますから、いすは この ままに して おいて ください。

Please leave the chairs as they are because a meeting will be held here tomorrow.

[Note] In daily conversation, 〜て おきます often becomes 〜ときます.

⑬ そこに 置いといて (置いて おいて) ください。

Please leave it there.

3.　｜ まだ V (affirmative) ｜　　still V

⑭ まだ 雨が 降って います。　　　　It's still raining.

⑮ 道具を 片づけましょうか。

…まだ 使って いますから、その ままに して おいて ください。

Shall I put away the tools?

…No, leave them there. I'm still using them.

まだ in ⑭ and ⑮ means "as yet" or "still" and indicates that the action or the state is continuing.

4. それは 〜　　that's

⑯ ブロードウェイで ミュージカルを 見たいと 思うんですが……。

…それは いいですね。

I'd like to see a musical on Broadway....

…That sounds nice.

⑰ 来月から 大阪の 本社に 転勤なんです。

…それは おめでとう ございます。

I will be transferred to the Osaka head office next month.

…Congratulations!　　　　　　　　　　　　　　　　　(L. 31)

⑱ 時々 頭や 胃が 痛く なるんです。

…それは いけませんね。

Sometimes I have pains in my stomach and head.

…That's bad.　　　　　　　　　　　　　　　　　　　(L. 32)

それ in ⑯, ⑰ and ⑱ refers to what is stated just before.

Lesson 31

I.   Vocabulary

はじまります Ⅰ [しきが〜]	始まります [式が〜]	[a ceremony] begin, start
★ つづけます Ⅱ	続けます	continue
★ みつけます Ⅱ	見つけます	find
★ うけます Ⅱ [しけんを〜]	受けます [試験を〜]	take [an examination]
にゅうがくします Ⅲ [だいがくに〜]	入学します [大学に〜]	enter [a university]
★ そつぎょうします Ⅲ [だいがくを〜]	卒業します [大学を〜]	graduate [from a university]
★ しゅっせきします Ⅲ [かいぎに〜]	出席します [会議に〜]	attend [a meeting]
きゅうけいします Ⅲ	休憩します	take a break, take a rest
れんきゅう	連休	consecutive holidays
さくぶん	作文	essay, composition
てんらんかい	展覧会	exhibition
けっこんしき	結婚式	wedding ceremony
[お]そうしき	[お]葬式	funeral
しき	式	ceremony
ほんしゃ	本社	head office
してん	支店	branch office
きょうかい	教会	church
だいがくいん	大学院	graduate school
どうぶつえん	動物園	zoo
おんせん	温泉	hot spring, spa
おきゃく[さん]	お客[さん]	visitor, guest, customer, client
だれか		somebody
★〜の ほう	〜の 方	place toward 〜, direction of 〜

★ ずっと   all the time

※ピカソ   Pablo Picasso, Spanish painter (1881-1973)

※上野公園   Ueno Park (in Tokyo)

◀会 話▶

★ 残ります Ⅰ   remain, be left

月に   per month

普通の   ordinary, common, usual

インターネット   Internet

―― 読み物 ――

村   village

映画館   movie theater

嫌[な]   hateful, disagreeable

空   sky

閉じます Ⅱ   close

都会   city

子どもたち   children

★ 自由に   freely

★ 世界中   all over the world

集まります Ⅰ   gather

美しい   beautiful

★ 自然   nature

すばらしさ   goodness, virtue

★ 気が つきます Ⅰ   notice, become aware of

II. Translation

Sentence Patterns

1. Let's have a drink together.
2. I'm thinking of establishing my own company in the future.
3. I intend to buy a car next month.

Example Sentences

1. We are tired. Shall we take a rest?
   ···Yes, let's.
2. What are you going to do on New Year's Day?
   ···I'm thinking of going to a spa with my family.
   That sounds good.
3. Have you already completed your report?
   ···No, I haven't written it yet.
   I'm thinking of finishing it by this Friday.
4. Hans, are you going to continue with judo even after going back to your country?
   ···Yes, I intend to continue with it.
5. Won't you go home during the summer vacation?
   ···No. I will take a graduate school entrance exam, so I don't intend to go back.

6. I go to New York on a business trip from tomorrow.
   ···Is that so? When will you come back?
   I'm scheduled to come back next Friday.

Conversation

I think I will start using the Internet

Ogawa: I will be single from next month.
Miller: What?
Ogawa: Actually I will be transferred to the Osaka head office.
Miller: The head office? Congratulations!
But, why are you going to be single?
Ogawa: My wife and son will stay in Tokyo.
Miller: Won't they go with you?
Ogawa: My son says that he wants to stay in Tokyo because he will take a university entrance exam next year. And my wife doesn't want to quit her job, either.
Miller: Well, are you going to live separately?
Ogawa: Yes, but I intend to come home at weekends a few times a month.
Miller: That's tough.
Ogawa: But, I have free time on weekdays, so I think I will start using the Internet.
Miller: I see. That's a good idea.

III. Reference Words & Information

専門　FIELDS OF STUDY

fukusenko : minor

医学	medical science	政治学	politics
薬学	pharmacology	国際関係学	international relations
化学	chemistry	法律学	law
生化学	biochemistry	経済学	economics
生物学	biology	経営学	business administration
農学	agriculture	社会学	sociology
地学	geology	教育学	education
地理学	geography	文学	literature
数学	mathematics	言語学	linguistics
物理学	physics	心理学	psychology
工学	engineering	哲学	philosophy
土木工学	civil engineering	宗教学	theology
電子工学	electronics	芸術	arts
電気工学	electrical engineering	美術	fine arts
機械工学	mechanical engineering	音楽	music
コンピューター工学	computer science	体育学	physical education
遺伝子工学	genetic engineering		
建築学	architecture		
天文学	astronomy		
環境科学	environmental science		

IV. Grammar Explanation

1. Volitional form

The volitional form of verbs is made as follows. (See Main Textbook, Lesson 31, p. 46, 練習A1.)

Group I ： Replace the last sound of the ます-form with the sound in the お-line of the same row and attach う.

Group II ： Attach よう to the ます-form.

Group III ： します becomes しよう, and きます becomes こよう.

2. How to use the volitional form

1) In plain style sentences

The volitional form is used instead of 〜ましょう in plain style sentences.

① ちょっと 休まない？　　　　　　Shall we take a rest?

…うん、休もう。　　　　　　　…Yes, let's.

② 少し 休もうか。　　　　　　　　How about taking a rest for a while?

③ 手伝おうか。　　　　　　　　　Shall I help you?

[Note] As you see in ② and ③, か at the end of the sentences is not dropped though they are plain style sentences.

2) | V volitional form と 思って います |

This sentence pattern is used to express what the speaker is thinking of doing. V volitional form と おもいます can also express a similar meaning. V volitional form と おもって います implies that the speaker's decision was made some time ago.

④ 週末は 海に 行こうと 思って います。

I'm thinking of going to the beach at the weekend.

⑤ 今から 銀行へ 行こうと 思います。

I'm going to the bank now.

[Note] V volitional form と おもって います can be used to express a third person's will or intention.

⑥ 彼は 外国で 働こうと 思って います。

He is thinking of working in a foreign country.

3. | V dictionary form / V ない-form ない | つもりです |

V dictionary form つもりです is used to express the speaker's intention of doing something, and V ない-form ない つもりです is used to express the speaker's intention of not doing something.

⑦ 国へ 帰っても、柔道を 続ける つもりです。

Even when I go back to my country, I'll continue with my judo.

⑧ あしたからは たばこを 吸わない つもりです。

I'm determined not to smoke from tomorrow.

[Note] Compared with V volitional form と おもって います, V dictionary form つもりです sounds more determined.

4. | V dictionary form
N の } 予定です

By using this sentence pattern, you can inform people of schedules.

⑨ 7月の 終わりに ドイツへ 出張する 予定です。

I'm scheduled to go on a business trip to Germany at the end of July.

⑩ 旅行は 1週間ぐらいの 予定です。

The trip is scheduled to last for a week.

5. | まだ V て-form いません

This sentence pattern means that something has not taken place or has not been done yet.

⑪ 銀行は、まだ 開いて いません。   The bank is not open yet.

⑫ レポートは もう 書きましたか。   Have you written the report yet?

   …いいえ、まだ 書いて いません。   …No, not yet.

6. こ～／そ～

In writing, a demonstrative belonging to the そ-series is used when a word(s) or a sentence(s) mentioned before is referred to. Sometimes, however, a demonstrative belonging to the こ-series is used instead. In this case, the writer wants to describe something to the reader as though it really existed then and there.

⑬ 東京に ない 物が 1つだけ ある。それは 美しい 自然だ。

There's one thing missing in Tokyo. And that's nature.

⑭ わたしが いちばん 欲しい 物は 「どこでも ドア」です。この ドアを 開けると、どこでも 行きたい 所へ 行けます。

What I want most is a "magic door." When you open this door, you can go anywhere you want.   (L. 27)

Lesson 32

I. Vocabulary

うんどうします Ⅲ	運動します	take exercise
せいこうします Ⅲ	成功します	succeed
しっぱいします Ⅲ ［しけんに～］	失敗します ［試験に～］	fail [an examination]
ごうかくします Ⅲ ［しけんに～］	合格します ［試験に～］	pass [an examination]
もどります Ⅰ	戻ります	return
やみます Ⅰ ［あめが～］	 ［雨が～］	[rain] stop
はれます Ⅱ	晴れます	clear up
くもります Ⅰ	曇ります	get cloudy
ふきます Ⅰ ［かぜが～］	吹きます ［風が～］	[wind] blow
なおります Ⅰ ［びょうきが～］ ［こしょうが～］	治ります、直ります ［病気が～］ ［故障が～］	 recover from [sickness], get well be fixed, be repaired
つづきます Ⅰ ［ねつが～］	続きます ［熱が～］	[high temperature] continue
ひきます Ⅰ ［かぜを～］		catch [a cold]
ひやします Ⅰ	冷やします	cool
しんぱい［な］	心配［な］	worried, anxious
じゅうぶん［な］	十分［な］	enough, sufficient
おかしい		strange, funny
うるさい		noisy
やけど		burning（～を します：get burned）
けが		injury（～を します：get injured）
せき		cough（～が でます：have a cough）
インフルエンザ		influenza
そら	空	sky
たいよう	太陽	sun
ほし	星	star
つき	月	moon
かぜ	風	wind

きた	北	north
みなみ	南	south
にし	西	west
ひがし	東	east
すいどう	水道	faucet, tap, water supply
エンジン		engine
チーム		team
こんや	今夜	this evening
ゆうがた	夕方	late afternoon
まえ		a time in the past, before
おそく	遅く	late (time)
こんなに		like this
そんなに		like that (concerning a matter related to the listener)
あんなに		like that (concerning a matter not related to the speaker or the listener), that much
もしかしたら		possibly, perhaps
それは いけませんね。		That's too bad.
※オリンピック		Olympic Games

◁会話▷

元気 <small>げんき</small>	vigor
胃 <small>い</small>	stomach
働きすぎ <small>はたら</small>	working too much
ストレス	stress
無理を します Ⅲ <small>むり</small>	work more than one's capacity
ゆっくり します Ⅲ	take one's time

····· 読み物 ·····

星占い <small>ほしうらな</small>	horoscope
牡牛座 <small>おうしざ</small>	Taurus
困ります Ⅰ <small>こま</small>	be in trouble, have a problem
宝くじ <small>たから</small>	lottery
当たります ［宝くじが〜］ Ⅰ <small>あ　　　たから</small>	win [a lottery]
健康 <small>けんこう</small>	health
恋愛 <small>れんあい</small>	romantic love
恋人 <small>こいびと</small>	sweetheart, boyfriend, girlfriend
［お］金持ち <small>かね も</small>	rich person

II. Translation

Sentence Patterns

1. You had better take exercise every day.
2. It will snow tomorrow.
3. I may not be in time for the appointment.

Example Sentences

1. Students these days spend a lot of time on recreation, don't they?
   ···Yes, they do. But I think they should have a variety of experiences while young.
2. I want to go to Europe on a month's tour. Would 400,000 yen be enough?
   ···It's enough, I think.
   But you had better not carry it in cash.
3. What will happen to the Japanese economy?
   ···Well. It will not recover so soon.
4. Will the Olympic Games be successful?
   ···They surely will be.
   They have been preparing for them for a very long time.
5. Doctor, what's wrong with Hans?
   ···He has caught flu.
   He might have a high temperature for about three days, but don't worry.
6. Don't you think the engine has been making a strange noise?
   ···Yes. We might break down.
   Let's return to the airport immediately.

Conversation

You might be sick

Watanabe:	Mr. Schmidt, what's wrong with you? You don't look well.
Schmidt:	Recently I don't feel well.
	Sometimes I have pains in my stomach and head.
Watanabe:	That's too bad. You might be sick, so you should go and see a doctor.
Schmidt:	I think you're right.

Schmidt:	Doctor, what's wrong with me?
Doctor:	Nothing particularly bad.
	Are you busy with work?
Schmidt:	Yes. I work overtime a lot these days.
Doctor:	You work too much. Maybe you are stressed about work.
Schmidt:	I see.
Doctor:	You shouldn't push yourself too much.
	Take some leave and have a rest.
Schmidt:	I will.

III. Reference Words & Information

天気予報　WEATHER FORECAST
てんきよほう

晴れ（は）
clear, fair

曇り（くも）
cloudy

雨（あめ）
rain

雪（ゆき）
snow

晴れ（は）のち曇り（くも）
fine, cloudy later

曇り時々（一時）雨（くも　ときどき　いちじ　あめ）
cloudy, occasionally rain

曇り所によって雨（くも　ところ　あめ）
cloudy, partly rain

降水確率（こうすいかくりつ）
probability of rain

最高気温（さいこうきおん）
the highest temperature

最低気温（さいていきおん）
the lowest temperature

北海道地方（ほっかいどうちほう）
Hokkaido area

札幌（さっぽろ）

東北地方（とうほくちほう）
Tohoku area

仙台（せんだい）

長野（ながの）

中部地方（ちゅうぶちほう）
Chubu area

東京（とうきょう）

中国地方（ちゅうごくちほう）
Chugoku area

近畿地方（きんきちほう）
Kinki area

関東地方（かんとうちほう）
Kanto area

松江（まつえ）

大阪（おおさか）

名古屋（なごや）

高知（こうち）

四国地方（しこくちほう）
Shikoku area

鹿児島（かごしま）

九州地方（きゅうしゅうちほう）
Kyushu area

那覇（なは）

にわか雨（あめ）／夕立（ゆうだち）
shower

雷（かみなり）
thunder

台風（たいふう）
typhoon

虹（にじ）
rainbow

風（かぜ）
wind

雲（くも）
cloud

湿度（しつど）
humidity

蒸し暑い（むしあつい）
hot and humid

さわやか[な]
refreshing

IV. Grammar Explanation

1.
V た-form	
V ない-form ない	ほうが いいです

   ① 毎日 運動した ほうが いいです。

   It is good to do some exercise everyday.

   ② 熱が あるんです。

   …じゃ、おふろに 入らない ほうが いいですよ。

   I have got a fever.

   …So, you had better not take a bath.

   This pattern is used to make suggestions or to give advice. Depending on the situation, this expression may sound like you are imposing your opinion on the listener. Therefore, consider the context of the conversation carefully before using it.

   [Note] The difference between ～た ほうが いい and ～たら いい:

   ③ 日本の お寺が 見たいんですが……。

   …じゃ、京都へ 行ったら いいですよ。

   I would like to see some Japanese temples.

   …So, it would be a good idea to go to Kyoto.

   Example ③ illustrates a situation in which a simple suggestion is given. In such cases ～たら いい is used. ～た ほうが いい implies a comparison and a choice between two things even if it is not expressed in words.

2.
V	plain form	
い-adj	plain form	でしょう
な-adj	plain form	
N	～だ	

   This pattern expresses the speaker's inference from some information he/she has. When used in a question like ⑤, the speaker asks for the listener's inference.

   ④ あしたは 雨が 降るでしょう。

   It will rain tomorrow.

   ⑤ タワポンさんは 合格するでしょうか。

   Do you think Mr. Thawaphon will pass the exam?

3.
V	plain form	
い-adj	plain form	かも しれません
な-adj	plain form	
N	～だ	

   ～かも しれません also expresses the speaker's inference, and means that there is a possibility that some event or state occurred/occurs/will occur. The degree of certainty however is much lower than with ～でしょう.

   ⑥ 約束の 時間に 間に 合わないかも しれません。

   We might not be in time for the appointment.

4. きっと／たぶん／もしかしたら

1) きっと

This adverb indicates that the speaker is quite certain of what he/she is saying. The probability ranges from quite high to the same level as that of 〜でしょう.

⑦ ミラーさんは きっと 来ます。

Mr. Miller will surely come.

⑧ あしたは きっと 雨でしょう。

It will undoubtedly rain tomorrow.

2) たぶん

This adverb entails less certainty than きっと, and is mostly used with 〜でしょう. As shown in ⑩, たぶん is very often used with 〜と おもいます (see Lesson 21).

⑨ ミラーさんは 来るでしょうか。

…たぶん 来るでしょう。

Do you think Mr. Miller will come?

…I guess so.

⑩ 山田さんは この ニュースを たぶん 知らないと 思います。

I guess Mr. Yamada does not know this news.

3) もしかしたら

This adverb is used with 〜かも しれません in most cases. A sentence with もしかしたら expresses the idea that there is less of a possibility of some event or situation occurring (e.g., "I cannot graduate" in ⑪).

⑪ もしかしたら 3月に 卒業できないかも しれません。

There is a possibility I might be unable to graduate in March.

5. 何か 心配な こと

⑫ 何か 心配な ことが あるんですか。

Is anything bothering you?

As shown in ⑫, you cannot say しんぱいな なにか, but you should rather say なにか しんぱいな こと. Other similar examples are なにか 〜 もの, どこか 〜 ところ, だれか 〜 ひと, いつか 〜 とき, etc.

⑬ スキーに 行きたいんですが、どこか いい 所 ありませんか。

I want to go skiing. Could you recommend a good ski resort?

6. | Quantifier で |

で added to a quantifier indicates the limit of a price, time, quantity, etc., necessary for a state, an action or an event to be realized.

⑭ 駅まで 30分で 行けますか。

Can I reach the station in thirty minutes?

⑮ 3万円で ビデオが 買えますか。

Can I buy a video player for 30,000 yen?

Lesson 33

I. Vocabulary

にげます II	逃げます	run away
さわぎます I	騒ぎます	make a noise
あきらめます II		give up
なげます II	投げます	throw
まもります I	守ります	keep, follow, obey, protect
あげます II	上げます	raise, lift up
さげます II	下げます	lower, pull down
つたえます II	伝えます	convey (a message)
ちゅういします III	注意します	be careful [of the cars]
［くるまに〜］	［車に〜］	
はずします I	外します	be away [from one's desk]
［せきを〜］	［席を〜］	
だめ［な］		no good, not permitted, impossible
せき	席	seat
ファイト		fight
マーク		mark
ボール		ball
せんたくき	洗濯機	washing machine
〜き	〜機	〜 machine
きそく	規則	regulation, rule
しようきんし	使用禁止	Do not use.
たちいりきんし	立入禁止	Keep out.
いりぐち	入口	entrance
でぐち	出口	exit
ひじょうぐち	非常口	emergency exit
むりょう	無料	free of charge
ほんじつきゅうぎょう	本日休業	closed today
えいぎょうちゅう	営業中	open for business
しようちゅう	使用中	in use
〜ちゅう	〜中	〜 ing

どういう ～	what kind of ～
もう	(not) any longer (used with negatives)
あと ～	～ left

◁会話▷

駐車違反	parking violation
そりゃあ	well
～以内	within ～
警察	police station
罰金	fine

…… 読み物 ……

電報	telegram
人々	people
急用	urgent business
打ちます ［電報を～］ Ⅰ	send [a telegram]
電報代	telegram charge
できるだけ	as much as possible
短く	shortly, briefly
また	and
例えば	for example
キトク（危篤）	in a critical condition
重い 病気	serious illness
明日	tomorrow
留守	absence
留守番	looking after a house during the owner's absence
［お］祝い	celebration
亡くなります Ⅰ	pass away, die
悲しみ	sorrow, sadness
利用します Ⅲ	use

II. Translation

Sentence Patterns

1. Hurry.
2. Don't touch.
3. "Tachiiri-Kinshi" means "No Entry."
4. Mr. Miller said that he would go on a business trip to Osaka next week.

Example Sentences

1. It's no good. I can't run any more.
    ···Fight. You have 1,000 meters left.
2. We have no more time left.
    ···You have one minute more. Don't give up. Fight.
3. What is written there?
    ···It says "Tomare."
4. How do you read that kanji?
    ···"Kin'en."
    It means "Don't smoke."
5. What does this mark mean?
    ···It means that you can wash it in a washing machine.
6. Is Mr. Gupta there?
    ···He is out now. He said he would be back in about thirty minutes.
7. Excuse me, could you please tell Ms. Watanabe that the party tomorrow will be from six o'clock?
    ···All right. It starts at six o'clock, does it?

Conversation

What does this mean?

Watt:	Excuse me. I found this paper stuck on my car. How do you read this kanji?
University staff member:	It says "Chusha-Ihan."
Watt:	"Chusha-Ihan?" What does that mean?
Staff:	It means that you parked your car in a no-parking area. Where did you park your car, Professor Watt?
Watt:	I parked in front of the station. I went to the bookstore to buy a magazine; it only took 10 minutes.
Staff:	Well, parking in front of the station is not allowed even for 10 minutes.
Watt:	What is written here?
Staff:	It says that you must go to the police station within one week.
Watt:	Only that? Don't I have to pay a fine?
Staff:	Yes, you must pay 15,000 yen later.
Watt:	You're kidding. 15,000 yen?
	To think the magazine I bought only cost 300 yen.

33

III. Reference Words & Information

標識　SIGNS

営業中
Open for business

準備中
In preparation

閉店
Closed

定休日
Regular holiday

化粧室
Toilet

禁煙席
No smoking seat

予約席
Reserved seat

非常口
Emergency exit

火気厳禁
Flammable

割れ物注意
Fragile

運転初心者注意
Beginner driver

工事中
Under construction

塩素系漂白剤不可
Don't use chlorine

手洗い
Wash by hand

アイロン（低温）
Iron at a low
temperature

ドライクリーニング
Dry clean only

IV. Grammar Explanation

1. Imperative and prohibitive forms

meirei *kinshi* *kei*

1) How to make the imperative form of verbs (See Main Textbook, Lesson 33, p. 62, 練習 A1.)

Group I : Change the last sound of the ます-form into the sound of the え-line.

Group II : Attach ろ to the ます-form.

Group III: します becomes しろ and きます becomes こい.

[Note] Non-volitional verbs such as わかる, できる, ある, etc., do not have imperative forms.

2) How to make the prohibitive form of verbs (See Main Textbook, Lesson 33, p. 62, 練習 A1.)

With every verb, attach な to the dictionary form.

2. Use of the imperative and prohibitive forms

1) The imperative form is used to force a person to do something and the prohibitive form is used to command a person not to do something. Both the imperative and prohibitive forms have strong coercive connotations, so much so that the use of these forms alone or at the end of an imperative sentence is very limited. In colloquial expressions, the use of either form is, in most cases, limited to male speakers.

2) Both the imperative and prohibitive forms are used alone or at the end of a sentence in the following instances:

(1) By a man senior in status or age to a person junior to him, or by a father to his child. ← *not mother !*

① 早く 寝ろ。   Go to bed immediately.

② 遅れるな。   Don't be late.

(2) Between men who are friends. In this case, the particle よ is often attached at the end of the sentence to soften the tone.

③ あした うちへ 来い [よ]。   Come to my house tomorrow.

④ あまり 飲むな [よ]。   Don't drink too much.

(3) When there is not enough time to be very polite; e.g., when giving instructions to a large number of people in a factory or during an emergency, etc. Even in this case, they may be used only by men senior in status or age. *kinkyū*

⑤ 逃げろ。   Run. (*Escape*.)

⑥ エレベーターを 使うな。   Don't use the elevator.

(4) When a command is required during training many people or making students take exercise at schools and sports clubs.

⑦ 休め。   Rest.

⑧ 休むな。   Don't rest.

(5) When cheering at sporting events. In this case the expressions below are sometimes used by women as well. *ōen*

⑨ 頑張れ。   Fight!

⑩ 負けるな。   Don't lose!

(6) When a strong impact or brevity is required, as in a traffic sign or in a slogan.

⑪ 止まれ。   Stop.

⑫ 入るな。   Don't enter.

[Note] Ｖ ます-form なさい is another imperative style. It is used by parents to their children or by teachers to their students and is a little gentler than the imperative form. So women use this style instead of the imperative form. Yet it is not used when speaking to a senior.

mother → child

⑬ 勉強しなさい。　　　　　　　　Study.

3. 〜と 読みます and 〜と 書いて あります

⑭ あの 漢字は 何と 読むんですか。　　How do you read that kanji?

⑮ あそこに「止まれ」と 書いて あります。　"Tomare" is written over there.

と in ⑭ and ⑮ indicates the content in the same way as と of 〜と いいます (Lesson 21).

33

4. ┌─────────────────────┐
   │ X は Y と いう 意味です │　　"X" means "Y"
   └─────────────────────┘

This pattern is used to define the meaning of the word represented by "X." と いう comes from と いいます. The interrogative どういう is used to ask the meaning.

⑯「立入禁止」は 入るなと いう 意味です。　"Tachiiri-Kinshi" means don't enter.

⑰ この マークは どういう 意味ですか。　　What does this sign mean?

　…洗濯機で 洗えると いう 意味です。　　…It means machine washable.

5. ┌──────────────────────────┐
   │ "S"   │   │
   │ plain form │と 言って いました │
   └──────────────────────────┘

direct quotation
indirect

〜と いいました is used when quoting a third person's words (Lesson 21), while 〜と いって いました is used when conveying a third person's message.

w/o inflection - just repeating

51

⑱ 田中さんは「あした 休みます」と 言って いました。

message nuance

Mr. Tanaka said, "I will take a day off work tomorrow."

⑲ 田中さんは あした 休むと 言って いました。

Mr. Tanaka said that he would take a day off work tomorrow.

6. ┌──────────────────────────────┐
   │ "S"   │   │
   │ plain form │と 伝えて いただけませんか │
   └──────────────────────────────┘

These expressions are used when politely asking someone to convey a message.

⑳ ワンさんに「あとで 電話を ください」と 伝えて いただけませんか。

Could you please tell Mr. Wang to give me a call later?

㉑ すみませんが、渡辺さんに あしたの パーティーは 6時からだと 伝えて いただけませんか。

Could you please tell Ms. Watanabe that the party tomorrow will be from 6 o'clock?

Lesson 34

I.   Vocabulary

みがきます Ⅰ [はを～]	磨きます [歯を～]	brush [one's teeth], polish
くみたてます Ⅱ	組み立てます	assemble
おります Ⅰ	折ります	bend, fold, break, snap
きが つきます Ⅰ [わすれものに～]	気が つきます [忘れ物に～]	notice, become aware of [things left behind]
つけます Ⅱ [しょうゆを～]		put [in soy sauce]
みつかります Ⅰ [かぎが～]	見つかります	[a key] be found
します Ⅲ [ネクタイを～]		put on, wear [a tie]
しつもんします Ⅲ	質問します	ask a question
ほそい	細い	thin (of small diameter)
ふとい	太い	thick (of large diameter)
ぼんおどり	盆踊り	Bon Festival dance
スポーツクラブ		sports club
かぐ	家具	furniture
キー		key
シートベルト		seat belt
せつめいしょ	説明書	explanatory pamphlet, instruction book
ず	図	figure, drawing
せん	線	line
やじるし	矢印	arrow (sign)
くろ	黒	black (noun)
しろ	白	white (noun)
あか	赤	red (noun)
あお	青	blue (noun)
こん	紺	navy blue, dark blue (noun)
きいろ	黄色	yellow (noun)
ちゃいろ	茶色	brown (noun)

しょうゆ	soya, soy sauce
ソース	sauce, Worcestershire sauce
～か ～	～ or ～
ゆうべ	last night
さっき	a short while ago

◀会話▶

茶道	tea ceremony
お茶を たてます Ⅱ	make green tea
先に	first (when doing something before something else)
載せます Ⅱ	place on, load onto
これで いいですか。	Is this all right?
苦い	bitter

―― 読み物 ――――――――――――――――――――――――――――

親子どんぶり	a bowl of cooked rice with chicken and egg
材料	material, ingredient
－分	portion for ～ (used for indicating quantity)
鳥肉	chicken
－グラム	－ gram
－個	(counter for small objects)
たまねぎ	onion
4分の1　$\left(\frac{1}{4}\right)$	one fourth
調味料	seasoning, flavoring
なべ	pan, pot
火	fire, heating
火に かけます Ⅱ	put on the stove
煮ます Ⅱ	cook, boil
煮えます Ⅱ	be cooked, be boiled
どんぶり	ceramic bowl

II. Translation

Sentence Patterns

1. Please write down what I say from now.
2. I brush my teeth after eating.
3. I drink coffee without sugar.

Example Sentences

1. Everybody, let's practice the Bon Festival dance.
   ···Yes.
   Please dance as I do.
2. I had an interesting dream.
   ···What kind of dream was it? Tell me exactly what you dreamed.
3. This table, should I assemble it by myself?
   ···Yes, assemble it according to the instructions. It's easy.
4. Where did you lose your wallet?
   ···I don't know. I only noticed after I had come home.
5. Won't you come for a drink after work?
   ···I am sorry but it's my day to go to the sports club.
6. What should I wear to my friend's wedding?
   ···Well, in Japan, men go to a wedding dressed in a black or a dark blue suit and a white tie.
7. Should I eat this with soy sauce?
   ···No, please eat it without anything.
8. You have got a little slimmer, haven't you? Were you on a diet?
   ···No. I walk to the station instead of taking a bus.

Conversation

Please do as I do

Klara: I would like to see the tea ceremony.

Watanabe: Then, won't you come with me next Saturday?

Tea ceremony
instructor: Ms. Watanabe, make the tea, please.
Klara, have the cake first, please.

Klara: Oh, should I eat the cake first?

Instructor: Yes. When you drink tea after eating sweet cake, it tastes delicious.

Klara: Is that so?

Instructor: Well, let's drink the tea.
Please do as I do.
First take the cup with your right hand and put it on your left palm.

Klara: Is this all right?

Instructor: Yes. Next, turn the cup around twice, and drink the tea.

Instructor: How do you like it?

Klara: It's a little bitter, but delicious.

III. Reference Words & Information

料理 COOKING
りょう り

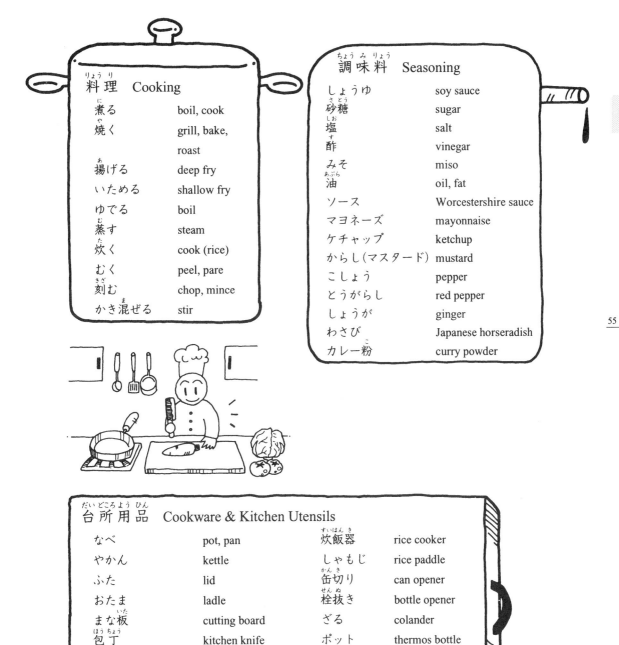

料理 Cooking
りょう り

煮る に	boil, cook
焼く や	grill, bake, roast
揚げる あ	deep fry
いためる	shallow fry
ゆでる	boil
蒸す む	steam
炊く た	cook (rice)
むく	peel, pare
刻む きざ	chop, mince
かき混ぜる	stir

調味料 Seasoning
ちょう み りょう

しょうゆ	soy sauce
砂糖 さ とう	sugar
塩 しお	salt
酢 す	vinegar
みそ	miso
油 あぶら	oil, fat
ソース	Worcestershire sauce
マヨネーズ	mayonnaise
ケチャップ	ketchup
からし(マスタード)	mustard
こしょう	pepper
とうがらし	red pepper
しょうが	ginger
わさび	Japanese horseradish
カレー粉 こ	curry powder

34

55

台所用品 Cookware & Kitchen Utensils
だいどころよう ひん

なべ	pot, pan	炊飯器 すいはん き	rice cooker
やかん	kettle	しゃもじ	rice paddle
ふた	lid	缶切り かん き	can opener
おたま	ladle	栓抜き せん ぬ	bottle opener
まな板 いた	cutting board	ざる	colander
包丁 ほうちょう	kitchen knife	ポット	thermos bottle
ふきん	kitchen towel	ガス台 だい	gas stove
フライパン	frying pan	流し[台] なが だい	sink
電子オーブンレンジ でん し	microwave oven	換気扇 かん きせん	ventilation fan

IV. Grammar Explanation

1.

| V₁ dictionary form
V₁ た-form
Nの | とおりに、V₂ |

1) | V₁ とおりに、V₂ |

This means to copy exactly in words or actions (V₂) what one has heard, seen, read or learnt, etc. (V₁).

① わたしが やる とおりに、やって ください。
　　Please do as I do.

② わたしが 言う とおりに、書いて ください。
　　Please write down what I say as it is.

③ 見た とおりに、話して ください。
　　Please tell us what you saw as it was.

The dictionary form is used when the action denoted by V₁ is going to be done from now, and the た-form is used when the action denoted by V₁ has already been done.

2) | Nの とおりに、V |

This means that an action (V) is done in accordance with the manner shown by the preceding phrase.

④ 線の とおりに、紙を 切って ください。
　　Please cut the paper following the line.

⑤ 説明書の とおりに、組み立てました。
　　I assembled it according to the handbook.

2.

| V₁ た-form
Nの | あとで、V₂ |

This sentence pattern means the action or occurrence denoted by V₂ takes place after the action or occurrence denoted by V₁ or N has taken place.

⑥ 新しいのを 買った あとで、なくした 時計が 見つかりました。
　　After I bought a new watch, I found the one I'd lost.

⑦ 仕事の あとで、飲みに 行きませんか。
　　Shall we go and have a drink after work?

Compared with V て-form から, which has a similar meaning, V た-form あとで emphasizes the time context in which the respective events happen.

3.

V_1 て-form V_1 ない-form ないで	V_2

V_1 is an action or condition which accompanies the action denoted by V_2. Look at ⑧ and ⑨. Using this pattern, whether soy sauce is used or not when the action たべます takes place is stated. V_1 and V_2 are actions done by the same person.

⑧ しょうゆを つけて 食べます。　　We eat it with soy sauce.

⑨ しょうゆを つけないで 食べます。　We eat it without soy sauce.

4.

V_1 ない-form ないで、 V_2

This pattern is used when the speaker indicates a course of action taken out of two alternative possibilities presented.

⑩ 日曜日は どこも 行かないで、うちで ゆっくり 休みます。

Next Sunday I won't go anywhere. I will rest at home instead.

Lesson 35

I. Vocabulary

さきます I [はなが～]	咲きます [花が～]	[flowers] bloom
かわります I [いろが～]	変わります [色が～]	[the color] change
こまります I	困ります	be in trouble, have a problem
つけます II [まるを～]	付けます [丸を～]	draw [a circle], mark [with a circle]
ひろいます I	拾います	pick up
かかります I [でんわが～]	 [電話が～]	get through [on the telephone], have [a phone call]
らく[な]	楽[な]	comfortable, easy
ただしい	正しい	correct, right
めずらしい	珍しい	rare, uncommon
かた	方	person (respectful equivalent of ひと)
むこう	向こう	over there, the other side
しま	島	island
むら	村	village
みなと	港	port, harbor
きんじょ	近所	neighborhood, vicinity
おくじょう	屋上	rooftop
かいがい	海外	overseas
やまのぼり	山登り	mountain climbing
ハイキング		hiking
きかい	機会	chance, opportunity
きょか	許可	permission
まる	丸	circle
そうさ	操作	operation
ほうほう	方法	method

せつび	設備	equipment, facilities
カーテン		curtain
ひも		string
ふた		lid, cover, cap
は	葉	leaf
きょく	曲	a piece of music
たのしみ	楽しみ	pleasure, enjoyment, expectation
もっと		more
はじめに	初めに	first

これで おわります。　これで 終わります。　We'll finish now.

※箱根	resort in Kanagawa Prefecture
※日光	tourist spot in Tochigi Prefecture
※白馬	resort in Nagano Prefecture
※アフリカ	Africa

◁会話▷

それなら	in that case
夜行バス	night bus
旅行社	travel agency
詳しい	detailed
スキー場	ski resort, ski ground
※草津	resort in Gunma Prefecture
※志賀高原	national park in Nagano Prefecture

····· 読み物 ·······

朱	red
交わります Ⅰ	keep company with
ことわざ	proverb
仲よく します Ⅲ	be on good terms with
必要[な]	necessary, essential

II. Translation

Sentence Patterns

1. Cherry blossoms bloom when spring comes.
2. When it is fine, an island can be seen over there.
3. For a trip to Hokkaido, June is a good season.
4. Where wedding speeches are concerned, the shorter they are, the better.

Example Sentences

1. I can't open the car window.
   ···If you push that button, it opens.
2. Do you have any other opinions?
   ···No, nothing in particular.
   If you don't have any, let's finish now.
3. How do you like the life in Japan?
   ···We have everything, and it is very convenient. But, I think it would be better if the cost of living were a little cheaper.
4. Do I have to hand in the report by tomorrow?
   ···If it is impossible, hand it in by this Friday.
5. I think I will travel for a few days. Could you recommend a good place?
   ···Hummm... I think Hakone or Nikko is good for a few days.
6. I want to borrow a book. What should I do?
   ···Ask the reception to make a card for you.
7. Ms. Yone Ogawa is very active, isn't she?
   ···Yes. The older she becomes, the more active she is.

Conversation

If you go to a travel agency, you can find out

Thawaphon:	Mr. Suzuki, I want to go skiing with friends during the winter vacation. Could you recommend a good ski resort?
Suzuki:	How many days?
Thawaphon:	About three days.
Suzuki:	In that case, I think Kusatsu or Shiga is good. They have hot springs, too.
Thawaphon:	How can I get there?
Suzuki:	You can go by JR, but if you take a night bus, you arrive early in the morning. It is more convenient.
Thawaphon:	Which is cheaper?
Suzuki:	I don't know. If you go to a travel agency, you can get more detailed information.
Thawaphon:	And I have no skis or skiwear.
Suzuki:	You can rent everything at the ski ground. If you're worried though, you can reserve everything at the travel agency.
Thawaphon:	I see. Thank you very much.

III. Reference Words & Information

ことわざ　PROVERBS

住めば都
Wherever you live, once you get used to living there, it becomes home.

三人寄れば文殊の知恵
Two heads are better than one.
The more people there are, the better the idea that might occur.

立てばしゃくやく、座ればぼたん、
　　　　　歩く姿はゆりの花
She is very beautiful. A standing figure is like a peony, a sitting figure is like a tree peony and a walking figure is like a lily.

61

ちりも積もれば山となる
Many a little makes a mickle.
Even though it is small like dust, it becomes big like a mountain when piled up.

うわさをすれば影
Speak of the devil and he is sure to appear.
When you talk about someone, he will appear.

花よりだんご
Cake before flowers.
Substance rather than appearance.

転石苔を生ぜず　*A rolling stone gathers no moss.*

It can be interpreted in two ways.
① Those who are active make progress.
② Those who easily get tired and change their jobs can not succeed in life.

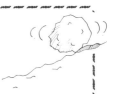

IV. Grammar Explanation

1. How to make the conditional form (See Main Textbook, Lesson 35, p. 78, 練習 A1.)

   Verb

   Group Ⅰ : Change the last sound of the ます-form into the sound of the え-line and attach ば.

   Group Ⅱ : Attach れば to the ます-form.

   Group Ⅲ : きます becomes くれば, and します becomes すれば.

   い-adj : Change the last い of the い-adjective into ければ.

   な-adj : Delete the last な of the な-adjective and attach なら.

   Noun : Attach なら to the noun.

2. | **Conditional form、～** |

   With the use of the conditional form, the former part of the sentence describes the requirements needed for an event or occurrence to manifest itself.

   When the subject of the former part is the same as that of the latter, you cannot use verbs containing volition in both parts of the sentence at the same time.

   1) When describing the requirements needed for a certain event to manifest itself:

   ① ボタンを 押せば、窓が 開きます。

   If you push the button, the window will open.

   ② 彼が 行けば、わたしも 行きます。

   If he goes, I will go, too.

   ③ いい 天気なら、向こうに 島が 見えます。

   When it is fine, an island can be seen over there.

   2) When describing the speaker's judgement on what the other person has said or the situation:

   ④ ほかに 意見が なければ、これで 終わりましょう。

   If you don't have any other opinions, let's close this meeting now.

   ⑤ あしたまでに レポートを 出さなければ なりませんか。

   …無理なら、金曜日までに 出して ください。

   Do I have to hand in the report by tomorrow?

   …If it is impossible, hand it in by this Friday.

[Note] Similar expressions that you have learned so far.

[1] ～と （Lesson 23）

   ～と is used when the result derived from the action described before と is inevitable. It is a predictable event or an unavoidable fact. ～と cannot be used when it comes to the speaker's wishes, judgement, permission, hopes, requests, etc.

   ⑥ ここを 押すと、ドアが 開きます。

   Press here, and the door will open.

   ⑥ can also be said using ～ば.

   ⑦ ここを 押せば、ドアが 開きます。

   If you press here, the door will open.

[2] ～たら （Lesson 25）

   As you learned in Lesson 25, ～たら has two usages: (1) it is a conditional expression, and (2) it indicates that an action or state will occur or appear when certain conditions have been met.

⑧ 時間が なかったら、テレビを 見ません。

    If I don't have time, I will not watch television.

⑨ 時間が なければ、テレビを 見ません。

    If I don't have time, I will not watch television.

× 時間が ないと、テレビを 見ません。

⑩ 東京へ 来たら、ぜひ 連絡して ください。

    Please contact me, when you come to Tokyo.

× 東京へ 来れば、ぜひ 連絡して ください。

In ⑧ and ⑨, ～たら and ～ば can be used, as unlike ～と, they are followed by expressions reflecting the speaker's will. In ⑩, however, only ～たら may be used because the subjects in the former and the latter denote the same person and both verbs are volitional. Although ～たら has the widest range of use, as is shown above, it is not usually used in newspaper articles and business reports because it is colloquial.

35

3. | Nなら、～ |

Nなら is also used when the speaker takes up the topic introduced by the other person and gives some information on it.

⑪ 温泉に 行きたいんですが、どこか いい 所 ありませんか。

    …温泉なら、白馬が いいですよ。

    I want to visit a hot spring resort. Don't you know any good place?

    …If you are talking about hot springs, Hakuba would be good.

63

4. | Interrogative　V conditional form　いいですか |

This expression is used to ask for directions or suggestions as to the best course of action. It is used in the same way as ～たら いいですか that you learned in Lesson 26. Hence, ⑫ can be restated as ⑬.

⑫ 本を 借りたいんですが、どう すれば いいですか。

    I would like to borrow some books. What should I do?

⑬ 本を 借りたいんですが、どう したら いいですか。

    I would like to borrow some books. What should I do?　　　　　　　　　(L. 26)

5.

V い-adj な-adj	conditional form	V dictionary form い-adj（～い） な-adjな	ほど ～

⑭ ビートルズの 音楽は 聞けば 聞くほど 好きに なります。

    The more I listen to the music of the Beatles, the better I like it.

⑮ パソコンは 操作が 簡単なら 簡単なほど いいです。

    The easier the operation, the better the computer.

The same verb or adjective is used in front of both ば/なら and ほど in the same sentence. This pattern expresses that the degree described in the latter part of the sentence increases/decreases with the change of the degree described in the former.

35

63

Lesson 36

I. Vocabulary

とどきます Ⅰ [にもつが～]	届きます [荷物が～]	[parcels] be delivered
でます Ⅱ [しあいに～]	出ます [試合に～]	participate [in the game]
うちます Ⅰ [ワープロを～]	打ちます	type [on a word processor]
ちょきんします Ⅲ	貯金します	save money
ふとります Ⅰ	太ります	get fat
やせます Ⅱ		get slim, lose weight
すぎます Ⅱ [7じを～]	過ぎます [7時を～]	pass [7 o'clock]
なれます Ⅱ [しゅうかんに～]	慣れます [習慣に～]	get accustomed to [the customs]
かたい	硬い	hard, tough, solid
やわらかい	軟らかい	soft, tender
でんし～	電子～	electronic ～
けいたい～	携帯～	portable ～
こうじょう	工場	factory
けんこう	健康	health
けんどう	剣道	kendo (Japanese style fencing)
まいしゅう	毎週	every week
まいつき	毎月	every month
まいとし(まいねん)	毎年	every year
やっと		finally
かなり		fairly
かならず	必ず	without fail, by any means
ぜったいに	絶対に	absolutely (used with negatives)
じょうずに	上手に	well, skillfully
できるだけ		as much as possible
このごろ		these days

〜ずつ	〜 (some amount) per (some suit)
その ほうが 〜	That is more 〜
※ショパン	Chopin, Polish musician (1810-49)

◁会話▷

お客様	guest, customer
特別[な]	special
して いらっしゃいます	be doing (respectful equivalent of して います)
水泳	swimming
〜とか、〜とか	〜, 〜, and so on
タンゴ	tango
チャレンジします Ⅲ	challenge
気持ち	feeling, enthusiasm

…… 読み物 …………………………………………………………………………

乗り物	vehicle, means of transportation
歴史	history
－世紀	-th century
遠く	far, remote place
汽車	locomotive
汽船	steam boat
大勢の 〜	many (people)
運びます Ⅰ	carry, transport
飛びます Ⅰ	fly
安全[な]	safe
宇宙	space, universe
地球	earth
※ライト兄弟	Wright brothers, American pioneers in aviation
	Wilbur Wright (1867-1912)
	Orville Wright (1871-1948)

II. Translation

Sentence Patterns

1. I practice every day so that I can swim fast.
2. I've finally become able to ride a bicycle.
3. I try to keep a diary every day.

Example Sentences

1. Is that an electronic dictionary?
   ···Yes. I carry it so that I can check immediately when I hear an unfamiliar word.
2. What does that red circle on the calendar mean?
   ···That's garbage collection day. I mark it so that I don't forget.
3. Are you now accustomed to using a futon?
   ···Yes. I had a hard time sleeping at first, but now I can really sleep soundly on it.
4. Can you now play work by Chopin?
   ···No, not yet.
   I want to become able to play Chopin soon.
5. Since the factory was completed, we've been unable to swim here.
   ···Really? That's a shame, isn't it?
6. You don't eat sweets, do you?
   ···No. I try not to eat sweets as much as possible.
   That's better for your body.
7. The concert begins at six o'clock.
   Please be sure not to be late. If you are late, you won't be able to get in.
   ···Yes, okay.

Conversation

I make the effort to use my brain and body

Announcer:	Good afternoon, everybody. This is "Health Hour."
	Today's guest is Ms. Yone Ogawa who is 80 years old this year.
Ogawa Yone:	Hello.
Announcer:	You look well. Do you do anything special to keep fit?
Ogawa Yone:	I try to take exercise every day, and eat a variety of foods.
Announcer:	What kind of exercise?
Ogawa Yone:	Dancing, swimming, and....
	Recently I've become able to dance the tango.
Announcer:	Great. What about food?
Ogawa Yone:	I eat anything. I especially like fish.
	I make the effort to cook a different dish every day.
Announcer:	You really use your brain and body.
Ogawa Yone:	Yes. I think I'd like to go to France next year, so I've started to learn French.
Announcer:	It's important that we have many challenges in life.
	Thank you very much, I enjoyed talking with you.

III. Reference Words & Information

けんこう
健康　HEALTH

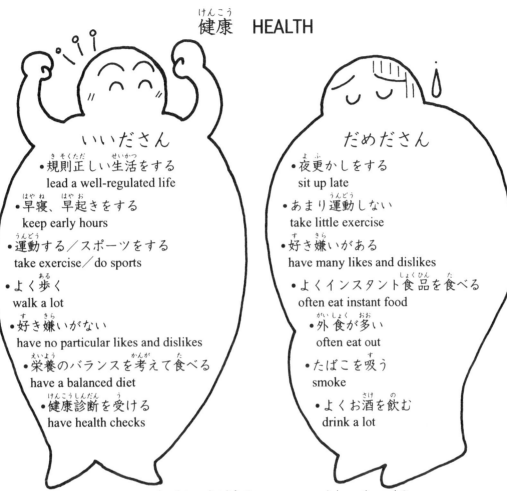

いいださん

- 規則正しい生活をする
きそくただ　　　せいかつ
  lead a well-regulated life
- 早寝、早起きをする
はやね　　はやお
  keep early hours
- 運動する／スポーツをする
うんどう
  take exercise／do sports
- よく歩く
ある
  walk a lot
- 好き嫌いがない
す　きら
  have no particular likes and dislikes
- 栄養のバランスを考えて食べる
えいよう　　　　　　かんが　　た
  have a balanced diet
- 健康診断を受ける
けんこうしんだん　う
  have health checks

だめださん

- 夜更かしをする
よ　ふ
  sit up late
- あまり運動しない
うんどう
  take little exercise
- 好き嫌いがある
す　きら
  have many likes and dislikes
- よくインスタント食品を食べる
しょくひん　た
  often eat instant food
- 外食が多い
がいしょく　おお
  often eat out
- たばこを吸う
す
  smoke
- よくお酒を飲む
さけ　の
  drink a lot

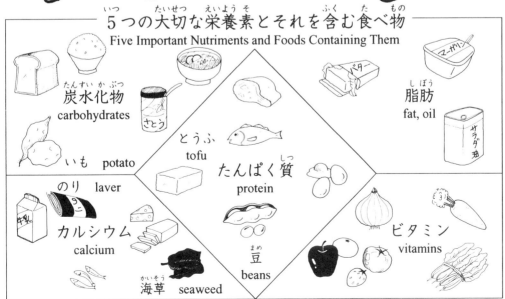

いつ　たいせつ　えいようそ　　　　　　　ふく　た　もの
５つの大切な栄養素とそれを含む食べ物
Five Important Nutriments and Foods Containing Them

たんすい か ぶつ
炭水化物
carbohydrates

さとう

いも　potato

脂肪
しぼう
fat, oil

バター

マーガリン

サラダ油

とうふ
tofu

たんぱく質
しつ
protein

のり　laver

牛乳

カルシウム
calcium

豆
まめ
beans

海草　seaweed
かいそう

ビタミン
vitamins

IV. Grammar Explanation

1. | V₁ dictionary form | ように、V₂ |
   | V₁ ない-form ない |

V₁ indicates a purpose or an aim, while V₂ indicates a volitional action to get closer to that objective.

① <u>速く 泳げるように</u>、<u>毎日 練習して います</u>。
　 aim　　　　　　　　　 (volitional) action

I practice every day so that I can swim fast.

② <u>忘れないように</u>、<u>メモして ください</u>。
　 purpose　　　　　　　 (volitional) action

Please take a memo so that you will not forget.

The dictionary form of non-volitional verbs such as potential verbs, わかります, みえます, きこえます, なります, etc., (①) or a verb in its negative form (②) should be used before ように.

2. | V dictionary formように | なります |
   | V ない-form なく |

1) なります indicates that a state changes into another state. The verbs used here express ability or possibility: such as potential verbs, わかります, みえます, etc. V dictionary formように なります indicates that a state in which something cannot be done has changed into a state in which it can be done. V ない-formなく なります indicates the reverse (i.e., something can no longer be done).

③ 毎日 練習すれば、泳げるように なります。

If you practice every day, you will become able to swim.

④ やっと 自転車に 乗れるように なりました。

I've finally become able to ride a bicycle.

⑤ 年を 取ると、小さい 字が 読めなく なります。

As you get older, you cannot read small letters.

⑥ 太りましたから、好きな 服が 着られなく なりました。

I gained weight so I can no longer wear my favorite dress.

2) How to give a negative answer to ～ように なりましたか is as follows:

⑦ ショパンが 弾けるように なりましたか。

…いいえ、まだ 弾けません。

Have you become able to play work by Chopin?

…No, not yet.

[Note] The Main Textbook does not discuss the usage shown in ⑧ and ⑨ on the next page. In this usage, using a verb which does not reflect ability will render the meaning that a habit which did not exist before has been acquired or a habit which existed before has become obsolete.

⑧ 日本人は 100年ぐらいまえから 牛肉や 豚肉を 食べるように なりました。

The Japanese started to eat beef and pork from about 100 years ago.

⑨ 車を 買ってから、わたしは あまり 歩かなく なりました。

I do not walk much since I bought a car.

Such verbs as なれる, ふとる, やせる, etc., which denote change itself cannot be used in this sentence pattern.

3.

V dictionary form V ない-form ない	ように します

This sentence pattern is used to express that one habitually or continuously makes efforts to do something or not to do something.

1) ～ように して います

This expresses that one habitually and continuously tries to do something.

⑩ 毎日 運動して、何でも 食べるように して います。

I try to take exercise every day and eat a variety of foods.

⑪ 歯に 悪いですから、甘い 物を 食べないように して います。

I try not to eat sweets because they are bad for my teeth.

2) ～ように して ください

～て／～ないで ください are direct request expressions, while ～ように して ください is an indirect request expression and more polite than the former. This pattern is used as shown below.

(1)When requesting someone to try to do something habitually and continuously.

⑫ もっと 野菜を 食べるように して ください。

Please try to eat more vegetables.

(2)When politely requesting someone to try to do something in a one-off situation.

⑬ あしたは 絶対に 時間に 遅れないように して ください。

Please be sure not to be late tomorrow.

[Note] ～ように して ください cannot be used when requesting something to be done on the spot.

⑭ すみませんが、塩を 取って ください。

Excuse me, please pass me the salt.

× すみませんが、塩を 取るように して ください。

4. とか

～とか is used to give examples just like ～や, but ～とか is more colloquial. Unlike や, とか sometimes comes after the last noun to be mentioned.

⑮ どんな スポーツを して いますか。

…そうですね。テニスとか 水泳とか……。

What kind of sports do you do?

…Well, playing tennis, swimming, and so on.

Lesson 37

I.　Vocabulary

ほめます　II	褒めます	praise
しかります　I		scold
さそいます　I	誘います	invite, ask someone to join
おこします　I	起こします	wake (someone) up
しょうたいします　III	招待します	invite
たのみます　I	頼みます	ask, request
ちゅういします　III	注意します	warn, advise
とります　I		rob, steal
ふみます　I	踏みます	step on (someone's foot)
こわします　I	壊します	break, destroy
よごします　I	汚します	make ～ dirty
おこないます　I	行います	hold, carry out, practice
ゆしゅつします　III	輸出します	export
ゆにゅうします　III	輸入します	import
ほんやくします　III	翻訳します	translate
はつめいします　III	発明します	invent
はっけんします　III	発見します	discover
せっけいします　III	設計します	design, plan
こめ	米	rice
むぎ	麦	barley, wheat
せきゆ	石油	oil
げんりょう	原料	raw material
デート		date
どろぼう	泥棒	thief, robber
けいかん	警官	policeman
けんちくか	建築家	architect
かがくしゃ	科学者	scientist
まんが	漫画	cartoon
せかいじゅう	世界中	all over the world
～じゅう	～中	all over ～
～に　よって		by ～
よかったですね。		That's lucky, isn't it?
※ドミニカ		Dominica

※ライト兄弟	Wright brothers, American pioneers in aviation
	Wilbur Wright (1867-1912)
	Orville Wright (1871-1948)
※源氏物語	"The Tale of Genji" (Japanese novel)
※紫式部	Heian Period (9th century) female novelist who wrote "The Tale of Genji" (973?-1014?)
※グラハム・ベル	Alexander Graham Bell, American inventor (1847-1922)
※東照宮	shrine dedicated to Tokugawa Ieyasu in Nikko, Tochigi Prefecture
※江戸時代	Edo Period (1603-1868)
※サウジアラビア	Saudi Arabia

◀会話▶

埋め立てます Ⅱ	reclaim
技術	technology, technique
土地	land
騒音	noise
利用します Ⅲ	use
アクセス	access

······ 読み物 ···

－世紀	-th century
豪華[な]	gorgeous
彫刻	engraving, carving, sculpture
眠ります Ⅰ	sleep
彫ります Ⅰ	engrave, carve
仲間	colleague, friend
その あと	after that
一生懸命	with all one's effort
ねずみ	mouse
一匹も いません。	There is not a single (mouse).
※眠り猫	The Sleeping Cat
※左 甚五郎	famous Japanese sculptor of the Edo Period (1594-1651)

II. Translation

Sentence Patterns

1. When I was a child I was often scolded by my mother.
2. My foot was trodden on in a rush-hour train.
3. Horyuji Temple was built in 607.

Example Sentences

1. This morning I was called in by the department manager.
   ···Did something happen?
   I was warned about how I write business trip reports.
2. What's wrong?
   ···Somebody has taken my umbrella by mistake.
3. A new star has been discovered.
   ···Really?
4. Where is this year's world conference of children to be held?
   ···It's to be held in Hiroshima.
5. What is sake made from?
   ···It's made from rice.
   What about beer?
   ···It's made from barley.
6. Which language is used in Dominica?
   ···Spanish is used there.
7. Teacher, who invented the airplane?
   ···The airplane was invented by the Wright brothers.

Conversation

Kansai Airport is made on reclaimed land

Matsumoto: Mr. Schmidt, is this your first visit to Kansai Airport?
Schmidt: Yes. It's really built on the sea, isn't it?
Matsumoto: Yes. This is an island reclaimed from the sea.
Schmidt: Amazing. What high technology.
But why did they build it on the sea?
Matsumoto: Because Japan has little space, and at sea we don't have a problem with noise pollution.
Schmidt: And that's why you can use it 24 hours a day.
Matsumoto: Yes.
Schmidt: This building has an interesting design.
Matsumoto: It was designed by an Italian architect.
Schmidt: Is access easy?
Matsumoto: It's one hour by train from Osaka Station.
You can also come from Kobe by sea.

III. Reference Words & Information

<ruby>事故<rt>じ こ</rt></ruby> ・ <ruby>事件<rt>じ けん</rt></ruby>   INCIDENT

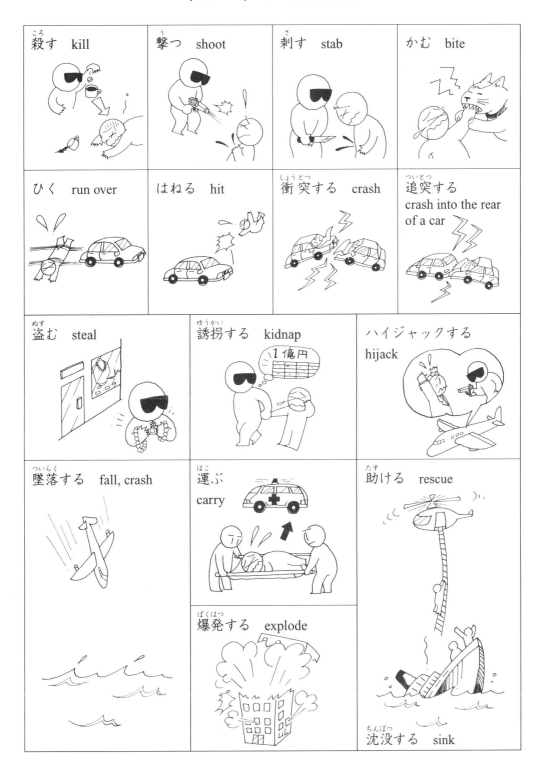

IV. Grammar Explanation

1. Passive verbs

How to make passive verbs (See Main Textbook, Lesson 37, p. 96, 練_{れん}習_{しゅう}A1.)

		Passive verbs	
		polite form	plain form
I	かきます	かかれます	かかれる
II	ほめます	ほめられます	ほめられる
III	きます	こられます	こられる
	します	されます	される

All passive verbs are Group II verbs; they conjugate into the dictionary form, ない-form, て-form, etc.

    e.g. かかれる, かかれ(ない), かかれて

2.   N₁(person₁)は N₂(person₂)に V passive

When a person (person₂)'s action is directed to another person (person₁), person₁ can state it from his/her side by using this sentence pattern. In this case, person₁ becomes the topic of the sentence, person₂ is marked with に, and a passive verb is used.

    先生_{せんせい}は わたしを 褒_ほめました。   My teacher praised me.

① わたしは 先生_{せんせい}に 褒_ほめられました。   I was praised by my teacher.

    母_{はは}は わたしに 買_かい物_{もの}を 頼_{たの}みました。

    My mother asked me to go shopping.

② わたしは 母_{はは}に 買_かい物_{もの}を 頼_{たの}まれました。

    I was asked to go shopping by my mother.

Something that moves (animals, cars, etc.) can replace person₂ in this sentence pattern.

③ わたしは 犬_{いぬ}に かまれました。   I was bitten by a dog.

3.   N₁(person₁)は N₂(person₂)に N₃ を V passive

When a person (person₂)'s action is directed to an object belonging to another person (person₁), and person₁ feels annoyed or troubled, person₁ uses this sentence pattern to express his/her feelings.

    弟_{おとうと}が わたしの パソコンを 壊_{こわ}しました。

    My brother broke my personal computer.

④ わたしは 弟_{おとうと}に パソコンを 壊_{こわ}されました。

    I had my personal computer broken by my brother.

Like in sentence pattern 2. above, an animate object or something that moves can replace person₂.

⑤ わたしは 犬_{いぬ}に 手_てを かまれました。 I had my hand bitten by a dog.

[Note 1] In this sentence pattern, the topic of the sentence is not the object (N₃) of the verb but person₁ (N₁), who feels annoyed or troubled by what person₂ does to the object belonging to him/her. Thus わたしの パソコンは おとうとに こわされました is not correct. You should use sentence ④ shown on the previous page instead.

[Note 2] As this sentence pattern is used when person₁ is troubled by what person₂ does, it cannot be used when person₁ is grateful for what person₂ does. 〜て もらいます is used instead.

⑥ わたしは 友達に 自転車を 修理して もらいました。

I had my bicycle repaired by my friend.

✕ わたしは 友達に 自転車を 修理されました。

4. ┃ N (thing) が／は　V passive

When you need not mention the person who does the action denoted by a verb, you can make the object of the verb the subject of the sentence. In this case, a passive verb is used.

⑦ フランスで 昔の 日本の 絵が 発見されました。

An old Japanese picture has been discovered in France.

⑧ 日本の 車は 世界中へ 輸出されて います。

Japanese cars are exported all over the world.

⑨ 会議は 神戸で 開かれました。

The assembly was held in Kobe.

5. ┃ N₁は　N₂(person) に よって　V passive

When something is created or discovered, and it is stated using a passive verb, the person who created or discovered it is indicated by に よって instead of に. Verbs like かきます, はつめいします, はっけんします, etc., are used in this sentence pattern.

⑩ 「源氏物語」は 紫式部に よって 書かれました。

"The Tale of Genji" was written by Murasaki Shikibu.

⑪ 電話は ベルに よって 発明されました。

The telephone was invented by Bell.

6. N から／N で つくります

When something is made from a raw material, the material is marked with から. When it is obvious to the eye that something is made of a particular material, the material is marked with で.

⑫ ビールは 麦から 造られます。

Beer is made from barley.

⑬ 昔 日本の 家は 木で 造られました。

Japanese houses were made of wood in the past.

Lesson 38

I. Vocabulary

そだてます Ⅱ	育てます	breed, bring up
はこびます Ⅰ	運びます	carry, transport
なくなります Ⅰ	亡くなります	pass away (euphemistic expression for しにます (L. 39))
にゅういんします Ⅲ	入院します	enter hospital
たいいんします Ⅲ	退院します	leave hospital
いれます Ⅱ 　［でんげんを～］	入れます 　［電源を～］	turn on [the power switch]
きります Ⅰ 　［でんげんを～］	切ります 　［電源を～］	turn off [the power switch]
かけます Ⅱ 　［かぎを～］	掛けます	lock
きもちが いい	気持ちが いい	pleasant, agreeable
きもちが わるい	気持ちが 悪い	unpleasant, disgusting
おおきな ～	大きな ～	large ～
ちいさな ～	小さな ～	small ～
あかちゃん	赤ちゃん	baby
しょうがっこう	小学校	elementary school
ちゅうがっこう	中学校	junior high school
えきまえ	駅前	the area in front of the station
かいがん	海岸	seaside, seashore
うそ		lie, fib
しょるい	書類	document, papers
でんげん	電源	power switch
～せい	～製	made in ～

[あ、] いけない。		Oops!/ Oh, no! (used when one has made a mistake)
おさきに　　　　　お先に 　[しつれいします]。　[失礼します]。		Excuse me (for leaving before you).

※原爆ドーム	dome commemorating the atomic bombing of Hiroshima

◀会話▶

回覧	circular, sending round
研究室	study room, professor's office, laboratory
きちんと	neatly, tidily
整理します Ⅲ	put (things) in order, tidy up
～という本	the book titled ～, the book named ～
一冊	(counter for books, etc.)
はんこ	seal stamp
押します [はんこを～] Ⅰ	affix [a seal]

······ 読み物 ···

双子	twins
姉妹	sisters
5年生	fifth grade, fifth year
似ています Ⅱ	resemble, be like
性格	character
おとなしい	quiet
世話を します Ⅲ	take care
時間が たちます Ⅰ	time pass by
大好き[な]	like very much
一点	－points
クラス	class
けんかします Ⅲ	quarrel, fight
不思議[な]	mysterious, strange

II. Translation

Sentence Patterns

1. Drawing pictures is fun.
2. I like looking at the stars.
3. I forgot to bring my wallet.
4. It was last March that I came to Japan.

Example Sentences

1. Are you still keeping a diary?
   ⋯No, I stopped after three days.
   It's easy to start, but it's difficult to continue.
2. What with all the flowers, it's a very beautiful garden, isn't it?
   ⋯Thank you.
   My husband is good at growing flowers.
3. How do you like Tokyo?
   ⋯Well, there are so many people. And they walk fast.
4. Oh, no!
   ⋯What's wrong?
   I forgot to close the car window.
5. Do you know that Ms. Kimura had a baby?
   ⋯No, I didn't. When was that?
   It was about a month ago.
6. Do you remember the person with whom you were in love for the first time?
   ⋯Yes. It was in my class at the elementary school where I saw her for the first time.
   She was a teacher of music.

Conversation

I like putting things in order

University
employee: Professor Watt, here's a circular.

Watt: Oh, thank you. Please leave it there.

Employee: Your office is always in perfect order, isn't it?

Watt: I like putting things in order.

Employee: The books are arranged well and everything is put to rights.... You are good at arranging things.

Watt: I once wrote a book titled "How to Arrange Things."

Employee: Oh, great!

Watt: It didn't sell well.
If you like, I will give you a copy.

Employee: Good morning.

Watt: Oh, I forgot to bring the book. I'm sorry.

Employee: Never mind. But, please don't forget to stamp the circular. You forgot last month, too.

III. Reference Words & Information

年中行事　ANNUAL EVENTS
ねん ちゅう ぎょう じ

1月1日〜3日
がつついたち　みっか

お正月　New Year's Day
しょう がつ

Celebration at the beginning of the year. People go to shrines or temples to pray for health and prosperity. New Year's cards arrive on New Year's Day.

3月3日
がつみっか

ひな祭り　The Doll's Festival
まつ

People who have a daughter display dolls.

5月5日
がついつか

こどもの日
ひ
Children's Day

Celebration for the growth and health of children. Originally, the day was set to celebrate the growth of boys.

7月7日
がつなのか

七夕　The Star Festival
たなばた

Based on a Chinese legend, Altair and Vega come from the eastern and western extremes of the Milky Way once a year to meet.

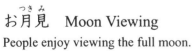
8月13日〜15日
がつ　にち　　にち

お盆
ぼん
The Bon Festival

The Bon Festival is a Buddhist tradition of greeting the spirits of deceased ancestors.
People visit the cemetery where their relatives are buried.

9月15日ごろ
がつ　にち

お月見　Moon Viewing
つき み

People enjoy viewing the full moon.

12月31日
がつ　にち

大みそか　New Year's Eve
おお

People prepare for the New Year, cooking 'osechi'(special food for New Year's Day) and cleaning the house.
At midnight the temple bells begin to ring.

IV. Grammar Explanation

1. ┌ V plain form の ┐

Attach the particle の to the plain form of a verb and you can nominalize the phrase accompanying that verb.

2. ┌ V dictionary form のは adjective です ┐

① テニスは おもしろいです。 Tennis is fun.

② テニスを するのは おもしろいです。 Playing tennis is fun.

③ テニスを 見るのは おもしろいです。 Watching tennis is fun.

① simply refers to tennis as a sport, while ② and ③ are more specific in referring to either playing or watching tennis. Such adjectives as むずかしい, やさしい, おもしろい, たのしい, きけん[な], たいへん[な], etc., are frequently used in this sentence pattern.

3. ┌ V dictionary form のが adjective です ┐

④ わたしは 花が 好きです。 I like flowers.

⑤ わたしは 花を 育てるのが 好きです。 I like growing flowers.

⑥ 東京の 人は 歩くのが 速いです。 People in Tokyo walk fast.

The adjectives which are used in this sentence pattern are usually ones that describe likes or dislikes and skills or capabilities such as すき[な], きらい[な], じょうず[な], へた[な], はやい, おそい, etc.

4. ┌ V dictionary form のを 忘れました ┐ forgot to do ...

⑦ かぎを 忘れました。 I forgot the key.

⑧ 牛乳を 買うのを 忘れました。 I forgot to buy the milk.

⑨ 車の 窓を 閉めるのを 忘れました。 I forgot to close the car window.

⑧ means the person "had to buy the milk, but forgot it." And ⑨ means the person "had to close the window of the car, but left the car with the window open."

5. ┌ V plain form のを 知って いますか ┐ Do you know that ... ?

This is an expression asking whether the listener knows what is described in the clause preceeding の.

⑩ 鈴木さんが 来月 結婚するのを 知って いますか。

　　Do you know that Mr. Suzuki is going to get married next month?

[Note] The difference between しりません and しりませんでした:

⑪ 木村さんに 赤ちゃんが 生まれたのを 知って いますか。

　…いいえ、知りませんでした。

　Do you know that Ms. Kimura had a baby?

　…No, I didn't.

⑫ ミラーさんの 住所を 知って いますか。

　…いいえ、知りません。

　Do you know Mr. Miller's address?

　…No, I don't.

しりませんでした is used in example ⑪, because the person replying has got the information from the question. In example ⑫, however, しりません is used because the person replying has not got any information from the question.

6.

V	plain form	
い-adj	plain form	
な-adj	plain form ～だ→～な	のは N です
N	～だ→～な	

　娘は 北海道の 小さな 町で 生まれました。

　My daughter was born in a small town in Hokkaido.

⑬ 娘が 生まれたのは 北海道の 小さな 町です。

　My daughter's birthplace is a small town in Hokkaido.

　12月は 1年で いちばん 忙しいです。

　December is the busiest month of the year.

⑭ 1年で いちばん 忙しいのは 12月です。

　The busiest month of the year is December.

This pattern is used when a noun representing a thing, a person, a place, etc., is replaced with の and then taken up as the topic of the sentence. In examples ⑬ and ⑭, "the place where my daughter was born" and "the busiest month of the year" are taken up as topics, and the speaker gives related information in the latter half of the sentence.

7. ～ときも／～ときや／～ときの／～ときに, etc.

Various particles can be attached to ～とき, which you learned in Lesson 23, because the word とき is a noun.

⑮ 疲れた ときや 寂しい とき、田舎を 思い出す。

　I remember my hometown when I am tired or lonely.　　　　　　　　(L. 31)

⑯ 生まれた ときから、ずっと 大阪に 住んで います。

　I have been living in Osaka since I was born.

Lesson 39

I. Vocabulary

こたえます II [しつもんに～]	答えます [質問に～]	answer [a question]
たおれます II [ビルが～]	倒れます	[a building] fall down
やけます II [うちが～] [パンが～] [にくが～]	焼けます [肉が～]	 [a house] burn down [bread] be baked [meat] be roasted, be grilled
とおります I [みちを～]	通ります [道を～]	pass [along a street]
しにます I	死にます	die
びっくりします III		be surprised
がっかりします III		be disappointed
あんしんします III	安心します	be relieved
ちこくします III	遅刻します	be late, come late
そうたいします III	早退します	leave (work or school) earlier than usual
けんかします III		quarrel, fight
りこんします III	離婚します	divorce
ふくざつ[な]	複雑[な]	complicated, complex
じゃま[な]	邪魔[な]	obstructive, in the way
きたない	汚い	dirty
うれしい		glad, happy
かなしい	悲しい	sad
はずかしい	恥ずかしい	embarrassed, ashamed
じしん	地震	earthquake
たいふう	台風	typhoon
かじ	火事	fire
じこ	事故	accident
[お]みあい	[お]見合い	interview with a view to marriage

39

82

でんわだい	電話代	telephone charge
～だい	～代	charge, fare, fee
フロント		front desk, reception desk
－ごうしつ	－号室	room number －
あせ	汗	perspiration (～を かきます: perspire)
タオル		towel
せっけん		soap
おおぜい	大勢	a great number of people

おつかれさまでした。お疲れさまでした。 Thank you for your hard work. (used to express appreciation for a colleague's or subordinate's work)

うかがいます。　伺います。 I'm coming. (humble way of saying いきます)

◁会話▷

途中で	on the way, in the midst of
トラック	truck, lorry
ぶつかります Ⅰ	bump, collide
並びます Ⅰ	stand in a queue, line up

‥‥‥ 読み物 ‥‥‥‥‥‥‥‥‥‥‥‥‥‥‥‥‥‥‥‥‥‥‥‥‥‥‥

大人	adult
洋服	Western clothes
西洋化します Ⅲ	be Westernized
合います Ⅰ	fit, suit
今では	now
成人式	coming-of-age celebration

II. Translation

Sentence Patterns

1. I was surprised to hear the news.
2. Because of the earthquake a building collapsed.
3. I don't feel well, so I'll go to a hospital.

Example Sentences

1. How was the "omiai"?
   ⋯I thought he looked good when I saw his photo, but I was disappointed when I saw him in person.
2. We are going on a hike this Saturday. Won't you come along with us?
   ⋯I'm sorry, but I can't make it that day.
3. How did you like that movie?
   ⋯The story was complicated, so I could not understand it well.
4. I'm sorry to be late.
   ⋯What happened?
   The bus was delayed by an accident.
5. Won't you come for a drink now?
   ⋯I am sorry, but I have something to do, so I have to leave now.
   Well, see you.
6. I sleep on a futon lately, and I find using it very convenient.
   ⋯What did you do with your bed?
   I gave it to a friend, because my room is small and it got in the way.

Conversation

I'm sorry to be late

Miller: Ms. Nakamura, I'm sorry I'm late.
Nakamura: What happened, Mr. Miller?
Miller: Actually, there was a traffic accident on my way here, and the bus was delayed.
Nakamura: An accident involving the bus?
Miller: No. A truck and a car collided at the intersection and the bus could not move.
Nakamura: That was bad.
   There was no call from you, so everybody was worried.
Miller: I wanted to call from the station, but many people were queuing at the telephones.... I'm sorry.
Nakamura: I see.
   Well, let's start the meeting.

III. Reference Words & Information

気持ち FEELINGS

うれしい　happy

楽しい
pleasant, enjoyable

寂しい　lonely

悲しい　sad

おもしろい
amusing, interesting

うらやましい
envious

恥ずかしい
embarrassed,
ashamed

懐かしい
dear, longed for

びっくりする
be surprised

がっかりする
be disappointed

うっとりする
be enchanted

いらいらする
be irritated

どきどきする
be scared

はらはらする
feel uneasy

わくわくする
be excited

IV. Grammar Explanation

1.
> V て-form
> V ない-form なくて
> い-adj (〜ⅳ)→〜くて | 〜
> な-adj [な]→で

In this sentence pattern, the first part of the sentence presents a cause and the second part presents the consequence produced by the cause. Unlike 〜から that you learned in Lesson 9, this pattern has many constraints over its usage.

1) The words which come in the latter part are limited to those words which do not contain volition:

(1) Verbs and adjectives to express feelings, such as びっくりする, あんしんする, こまる, さびしい, うれしい, ざんねんだ, etc.:

① ニュースを 聞いて、びっくりしました。　　I was surprised to hear the news.

② 家族に 会えなくて、寂しいです。　　I miss my family.

(2) Potential verbs and verbs to express states:

③ 土曜日は 都合が 悪くて、行けません。

　　Saturday is inconvenient for me, so I cannot come.

④ 話が 複雑で、よく わかりませんでした。

　　The story was complicated, so I could not understand it well.

(3) Situations in the past:

⑤ 事故が あって、バスが 遅れて しまいました。

　　The bus was delayed by an accident.

⑥ 授業に 遅れて、先生に しかられました。

　　I was late for the lesson, so I was scolded by my teacher.

2) Expressions containing volition (will, orders, invitation or request) are not used in the latter part of the sentence. When the latter part of the sentence contains volition, the phrase with て cannot be used and instead the phrase with から is used.

⑦ 危ないですから、機械に 触らないで ください。

　　It is dangerous, so please do not touch the machine.

× 危なくて、機械に 触らないで ください。

3) In this sentence pattern, the first part and the second part of the sentence are sequential events. In other words, the first part takes place first and the second part takes place after that.

⑧ あした 会議が ありますから、きょう 準備しなければ なりません。

　　The meeting will be held tomorrow, so we have to make preparations for it today.

× あした 会議が あって、きょう 準備しなければ なりません。

2. Nで

The particle で that you learn in this lesson indicates a cause. Nouns used in this case are those which indicate natural phenomena, happenings, events such as じこ, じしん, かじ, etc. As with the sentence pattern in 1. on the previous page, in this construction expressions containing volition are not used as predicates.

⑨ 地震で ビルが 倒れました。

Because of the earthquake, a building collapsed.

⑩ 病気で 会社を 休みました。　　　Because of illness, I took a day off work.

× 病気で あした 会社を 休みたいです。

3.

V	plain form	
い-adj	plain form	
な-adj	plain form	ので、〜
N	〜だ→〜な	

Like 〜から that you learned in Lesson 9, 〜ので indicates causes and reasons. While 〜から subjectively highlights a cause or a reason, 〜ので objectively presents a cause-and-effect relationship as a natural course of events. As the use of 〜ので softens the view of the speaker, leaving a weak impact on the listener, it is often used to express a reason gently, to ask for permission or to make an excuse.

⑪ 日本語が わからないので、英語で 話して いただけませんか。

I don't understand Japanese, so would you please speak in English?

⑫ 用事が あるので、お先に 失礼します。

May I leave now? I have something to do.

As it is a soft expression, it is not used with the imperative or the prohibitive forms.

⑬ 危ないから、機械に 触るな。

Don't touch the machine because it's dangerous.

× 危ないので、機械に 触るな。

[Note] ので is used with the plain form as shown above. In more polite expressions, however, it can be used with the polite form.

⑭ 用事が ありますので、お先に 失礼します。

(＝用事が あるので、お先に 失礼します。)

May I leave now? I have something to do.

4. 途中で

とちゅうで means "during" or "on the way to." It follows V dictionary form or Nの.

⑮ 実は 来る 途中で 事故が あって、バスが 遅れて しまったんです。

Actually, on my way here there was an accident and the bus was delayed.

⑯ マラソンの 途中で 気分が 悪く なりました。

I got sick during the marathon.

Lesson 40

I. Vocabulary

かぞえます II	数えます	count
はかります I	測ります、量ります	measure, weigh
たしかめます II	確かめます	confirm, make sure
あいます I	合います	[the size] fit
[サイズが～]		
しゅっぱつします III	出発します	depart
とうちゃくします III	到着します	arrive
よいます I	酔います	get drunk
きけん[な]	危険[な]	dangerous
ひつよう[な]	必要[な]	necessary
うちゅう	宇宙	space, universe
ちきゅう	地球	earth
ぼうねんかい	忘年会	year-end party
しんねんかい	新年会	New Year's party
にじかい	二次会	second party
たいかい	大会	mass meeting, convention
マラソン		marathon
コンテスト		contest
おもて	表	face, front
うら	裏	back (side)
へんじ	返事	reply
もうしこみ	申し込み	application
ほんとう		truth, fact
まちがい		mistake
きず	傷	defect, wound, scratch
ズボン		trousers
ながさ	長さ	length
おもさ	重さ	weight
たかさ	高さ	height
おおきさ	大きさ	size, scale
[－]びん	[－]便	flight, flight number
－ごう	－号	train number, typhoon number, etc.
－こ	－個	(counter for small objects)

40

88

ーほん（ーぽん、ーぼん）	ー本	(counter for long objects)
ーはい（ーぱい、ーばい）	ー杯	ー glass or cup of (counter for full cups, glasses, etc.)
ーキロ		ー kilograms, kilometers
ーグラム		ー grams
ーセンチ		ー centimeters
ーミリ		ー millimeters
〜いじょう	〜以上	not less than 〜, over 〜
〜いか	〜以下	not more than 〜, under 〜
さあ		well, let me see (used when unsure of something)
※ゴッホ		Vincent van Gogh, Dutch painter (1853-90)
※雪祭り		Snow Festival in Sapporo
※のぞみ		name of a Shinkansen train
※ＪＬ		Japan Airlines

◁会 話▷

どうでしょうか。	How is 〜? (polite way of saying どうですか)
クラス	class
テスト	test, examination
成績	performance, score, result
ところで	by the way
いらっしゃいます Ⅰ	come (respectful equivalent of きます)
様子	situation, condition, appearance

…… 読み物 ……………………………………………………………………………………

事件	incident, case
オートバイ	motorcycle
爆弾	bomb
積みます Ⅰ	load, pile up
運転手	driver
離れた	remote
が	but
急に	suddenly
動かします Ⅰ	start, operate, move
一生懸命	with all one's effort
犯人	suspect, criminal
手に 入れます Ⅱ	obtain, get
今でも	even now
うわさします Ⅲ	gossip

II. Translation

Sentence Patterns

1. Please check what time JL107 will arrive.
2. They can't tell yet whether or not typhoon No. 9 will come to Tokyo.
3. I would like to try seeing the earth from space.

Example Sentences

1. Where did you go for the second party?
   ···As I was drunk, I don't remember where we went.
2. Do you know how they measure the height of mountains?
   ···Well, no. How do they do it?
3. Do you remember when it was that we first met?
   ···I've forgotten such an old story.
4. Please tell us by the 20th whether or not you can attend the year-end party.
   ···All right.
5. What do they examine there?
   ···They examine whether or not the boarding passengers carry knives or something dangerous.
6. Excuse me. May I try this dress on?
   ···Certainly, in here please.

Conversation

I am worried if my son has made any friends or not

Klara: Ms. Ito, how is Hans doing at school?
I'm worried if he has made any friends or not.

Ito: He is all right.
Hans is popular with his classmates.

Klara: Is he? I'm glad to hear that.
How are his studies going? He says studying kanji is hard.

Ito: I give a kanji test every day. Hans gets good marks.

Klara: Does he? Thank you.

Ito: By the way, soon we'll have Sports Day. Is his father coming, too?

Klara: Yes.

Ito: I hope that you can see what your son is like at school.

Klara: All right. I would appreciate if you could help him enjoy his school life.

40

90

III. Reference Words & Information

単位・線・形・模様　MEASUREMENT, SHAPES & PATTERNS
（たんい・せん・かたち・もよう）

面積　Area
（めんせき）

cm²	平方センチメートル（へいほう）	square centimeter
m²	平方メートル（へいほう）	square meter
km²	平方キロメートル（へいほう）	square kilometer

長さ　Length
（なが）

mm	ミリ［メートル］	millimeter
cm	センチ［メートル］	centimeter
m	メートル	meter
km	キロ［メートル］	kilometer

体積・容積　Volume and Capacity
（たいせき・ようせき）

cm³	立方センチメートル（りっぽう）	cubic centimeter
m³	立方メートル（りっぽう）	cubic meter
ml	ミリリットル	milliliter
cc	シーシー	cc
ℓ	リットル	liter

重さ　Weight
（おも）

mg	ミリグラム	milligram
g	グラム	gram
kg	キロ［グラム］	kilogram
t	トン	ton

計算　Calculation
（けいさん）

$$1 + 2 - 3 \times 4 \div 6 = 1$$

たす	ひく	かける	わる	は（イコール）
plus	minus	multiply	divide	equal

線　Lines
（せん）

直線（ちょくせん）	straight line	———————
曲線（きょくせん）	curved line	∿∿
点線（てんせん）	dotted line	··············

形　Shapes
（かたち）

円（丸）（えん・まる）
circle

三角［形］（さんかく・けい）
triangle

四角［形］（しかく・けい）
square

模様　Patterns
（もよう）

縦じま（たて）
vertical stripes

横じま（よこ）
horizontal stripes

チェック
check

水玉（みずたま）
polka-dot

花柄（はながら）
floral print

無地（むじ）
plain

IV. Grammar Explanation

1.

$$\text{Interrogative} \left\{ \begin{array}{l} \text{V} \\ \text{い-adj} \\ \text{な-adj} \\ \text{N} \end{array} \right\} \begin{array}{l} \text{plain form} \\ \text{plain form} \\ \sim \mathit{だ} \end{array} \right\} \text{か、} \sim$$

A question with an interrogative is used as a component of a sentence in this sentence pattern.

① JL107便は 何時に 到着するか、調べて ください。

Please check what time JL107 will arrive.

② 結婚の お祝いは 何が いいか、話して います。

We are talking about what to give as a wedding present.

③ わたしたちが 初めて 会ったのは いつか、覚えて いますか。

Do you remember when it was that we first met?

2.

$$\left\{ \begin{array}{l} \text{V} \\ \text{い-adj} \\ \text{な-adj} \\ \text{N} \end{array} \right\} \begin{array}{l} \text{plain form} \\ \text{plain form} \\ \sim \mathit{だ} \end{array} \right\} \text{か どうか、} \sim$$

A question without an interrogative is used as a component of a sentence in this sentence pattern. Note that どうか is necessary after "plain form か."

④ 忘年会に 出席するか どうか、20日までに 返事を ください。

Please answer by the 20th whether you'll attend the year-end party or not.

⑤ その 話は ほんとうか どうか、わかりません。

I don't know whether the story is true or not.

⑥ まちがいが ないか どうか、調べて ください。

Please check if there are no mistakes.

In ⑥, not まちがいが あるか どうか but まちがいが ないか どうか is used because the speaker wants to confirm that there are no mistakes.

3. | V て-form みます |

This sentence pattern is used to show that the action denoted by the verb is a trial.

⑦ もう 一度 考えて みます。　　　　I'll think it over again.

⑧ 宇宙から 地球を 見て みたいです。

I want to see the earth from space (to know how it looks).

⑨ この ズボンを はいて みても いいですか。

May I try on this pair of trousers?

4. い-adj (〜い) → 〜さ

Change the final い of an い-adjective into さ, and you can transform the adjective into a noun.

e.g., 高い→高さ　　長い→長さ　　速い→速さ

⑩ 山の 高さは どうやって 測るか、知って いますか。

Do you know how to measure the height of a mountain?

⑪ 新しい 橋の 長さは 3,911メートルです。

The new bridge is 3,911 meters long.

5. ハンスは 学校で どうでしょうか。

〜でしょうか, which is used to ask a question whose answer the listener might be uncertain of, is also used to ask a question whose answer the listener is sure to be able to give. In this case, it is euphemistic and hence more polite.

40

Lesson 41

I.   Vocabulary

いただきます Ⅰ		receive (humble equivalent of もらいます)
くださいます Ⅰ		give (respectful equivalent of くれます)
やります Ⅰ		give (to a younger person or subordinate)
よびます Ⅰ	呼びます	invite
とりかえます Ⅱ	取り替えます	exchange
しんせつに します Ⅲ	親切に します	be kind to
かわいい		lovely, cute
おいわい	お祝い	celebration, gift (〜を します：celebrate)
おとしだま	お年玉	money given as a New Year's gift
[お]みまい	[お]見舞い	expression of sympathy, consolatory gift to a sick person
きょうみ	興味	interest ([コンピューターに] 〜が あります：be interested [in computers])
じょうほう	情報	information
ぶんぽう	文法	grammar
はつおん	発音	pronunciation
さる	猿	ape, monkey
えさ		feed, bait
おもちゃ		toy
えほん	絵本	picture book
えはがき	絵はがき	picture postcard
ドライバー		screwdriver
ハンカチ		handkerchief
くつした	靴下	socks, stockings
てぶくろ	手袋	gloves
ゆびわ	指輪	ring
バッグ		bag

そふ	祖父	(my) grandfather
そぼ	祖母	(my) grandmother
まご	孫	grandchild
おじ		(my) uncle
おじさん		(someone else's) uncle
おば		(my) aunt
おばさん		(someone else's) aunt
おととし		the year before last

◁会話▷

はあ	yes, I see
申し訳 ありません。	I'm sorry./Excuse me.
預かります Ⅰ	keep, receive (a thing) in trust
先日	the other day
助かります Ⅰ	be of help

----- 読み物 ....

昔話	old tale, folklore
ある 〜	a certain 〜, one 〜
男	man
子どもたち	children
いじめます Ⅱ	bully, abuse, ill-treat
かめ	turtle, tortoise
助けます Ⅱ	save, help
[お]城	castle
お姫様	princess
楽しく	happily, merrily
暮らします Ⅰ	live, lead a life
陸	land, shore
すると	and, then
煙	smoke
真っ白[な]	pure white
中身	content

II. Translation

Sentence Patterns

1. I received a book from Professor Watt.
2. My section chief corrected the errors in my letter.
3. My department chief's wife taught me the tea ceremony.
4. I made a paper airplane for my son.

Example Sentences

1. It's a beautiful plate, isn't it?
   ···Yes. Mr. Tanaka gave it to me for a wedding present.
2. Mum, may I give candies to that monkey?
   ···No. It is written over there that you must not feed it.
3. Have you ever been to see a sumo match?
   ···Yes. My boss took me with him the other day.
   It was very interesting.
4. Mr. Thawaphon, how did you enjoy your homestay during the summer vacation?
   ···It was pleasant. The whole family treated me very kindly.
5. What do you do for your children on their birthday?
   ···I invite their friends and give a party.
6. I'm afraid I don't understand how to use the new photocopier. I'd be grateful if you could show me.
   ···Yes, of course.

Conversation

Could you keep my parcel?

Miller:	Ms. Ogawa, I'd like to ask a small favour.
Ogawa Sachiko:	What is it?
Miller:	A department store will deliver a parcel to me this evening, but I've got to go out to do something.
Ogawa Sachiko:	I see.
Miller:	I'm very sorry, but could you take it in and keep it for me?
Ogawa Sachiko:	Certainly.
Miller:	Thank you. I'll come for it as soon as I get back.
Ogawa Sachiko:	I see.
Miller:	I'm sorry to bother you with this.

Miller:	Oh, Ms. Ogawa. Thank you very much for taking in that parcel the other day for me.
Ogawa Sachiko:	Not at all.
Miller:	It was a big help.

III. Reference Words & Information

便利情報 USEFUL INFORMATION

宅配便なら、ペンギン便!
If it's a home delivery, call Penguin!

旅行の荷物を家から空港まで配達します。
From home to the airport luggage delivery service.

学生や単身者の小さい引っ越しをします。
Can also do small moves for students or single persons.

☎ 03-3812-5566

泊まりませんか
Come and stay with us.

民宿 三浦
MIURA Guest House

安い、親切、家庭的な宿
Nice accommodation with friendly atmosphere and warm service at a reasonable price.

☎ 0585-214-1234

公民館からのお知らせ Community Center Information

月曜日	Mon.	日本料理講習会	Japanese cooking class
火曜日	Tue.	生け花スクール	Flower arrangement class
水曜日	Wed.	日本語教室	Japanese language class

＊毎月第3日曜日 on the 3rd Sun. of every month バザー Bazaar

☎ 0798-72-2518

便利屋 Helping Hands
☎ 0343-885-8854

何でもします!!
Leave anything and everything to us.

☆家の修理、掃除
house repairs, house cleaning

☆赤ちゃん、子どもの世話
baby sitting

☆犬の散歩
dog walking

☆話し相手
companion service

レンタルサービス
Rental Service

何でも貸します!!
Rent anything and everything.

- カラオケ　　karaoke sets
- ビデオカメラ　video cameras
- 着物　　　　Japanese kimono
- 携帯電話　　cellular phones
- ベビー用品　baby goods
- レジャー用品　recreational equipment
- 旅行用品　　travel goods

☎ 0741-41-5151

お寺で体験できます
You can try the following at our temple.

禅ができます　　　　　　zen meditation
精進料理が食べられます　vegetarian food

金銀寺　☎ 0562-231-2010

IV. Grammar Explanation

1. Expressions for giving and receiving

In Lessons 7 and 24, you learned expressions for the giving and receiving of things and actions. In this lesson, you will learn other expressions for giving and receiving things or actions but these reflect the relationship between the giver and the receiver.

1) | N₁に N₂を やります |

When the receiver is a person of lower social status or an animal or plant, やります is normally used. However, when the receiver is a person, あげます is often preferred in current Japanese.

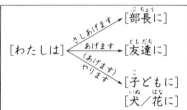

① わたしは 息子に お菓子を やりました（あげました）。

I gave some sweets to my son.

② わたしは 犬に えさを やりました。

I gave some food to the dog.

[Note] さしあげます is used when the speaker wants to show particular deference to the receiver.

2) | N₁に N₂を いただきます |

When the speaker receives a thing from a person of higher social status, いただきます is used instead of もらいます.

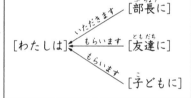

③ わたしは 部長に お土産を いただきました。

I received a souvenir from the general manager.

3) | ［わたしに］ Nを くださいます |

When a person of higher social status gives the speaker something, くださいます is used instead of くれます.

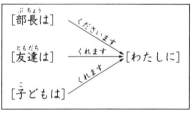

④ 部長が わたしに お土産を くださいました。

The general manager gave me a souvenir.

くださいます is also used when the receiver is a member of the speaker's family.

⑤ 部長が 娘に お土産を くださいました。

The general manager gave a souvenir to my daughter.

2. Giving and receiving of actions

やります, いただきます, and くださいます are also used in expressing the giving and receiving of actions. Examples are shown below.

1) | Vて-form やります |

⑥ わたしは 息子に 紙飛行機を 作って やりました（あげました）。

I made a paper plane for my son.

⑦ わたしは 犬を 散歩に 連れて 行って やりました。

I took my dog for a walk.

⑧ わたしは 娘の 宿題を 見て やりました（あげました）。

I checked my daughter's homework.

[Note] Like 〜て あげます, which you learned in Lesson 24, 〜て さしあげます may leave an impression of arrogance. So, it is advisable not to use these expressions directly to a person of higher social status.

2) | **V て-form いただきます** |

⑨ わたしは 課長に 手紙の まちがいを 直して いただきました。

I had my letter corrected by the manager.

3) | **V て-form くださいます** |

⑩ 部長の 奥さんは ［わたしに］ お茶を 教えて くださいました。

The general manager's wife taught me the tea ceremony.

⑪ 部長は ［わたしを］ 駅まで 送って くださいました。

The general manager took me to the station.

⑫ 部長は ［わたしの］ レポートを 直して くださいました。

The general manager corrected my report.

41

3. | **V て-form くださいませんか** |

〜て くださいませんか is a polite expression of request, although it is less polite than 〜て いただけませんか in Lesson 26.

99

⑬ コピー機の 使い方を 教えて くださいませんか。

Will you kindly show me how to use the photocopier?

⑭ コピー機の 使い方を 教えて いただけませんか。

Would you kindly show me how to use the photocopier?   (L. 26)

4. | **N に V** |

This particle に means "as a token of" or "in memory of."

⑮ 田中さんが 結婚の お祝いに この お皿を くださいました。

Mr. Tanaka gave this plate as my wedding gift.

⑯ わたしは 北海道旅行の お土産に 人形を 買いました。

I bought a doll as a souvenir of the trip to Hokkaido.

Lesson 42

I.   Vocabulary

つつみます Ⅰ	包みます	wrap
わかします Ⅰ	沸かします	boil
まぜます Ⅱ	混ぜます	mix
けいさんします Ⅲ	計算します	calculate
あつい	厚い	thick
うすい	薄い	thin
べんごし	弁護士	lawyer, attorney
おんがくか	音楽家	musician
こどもたち	子どもたち	children
ふたり	二人	couple
きょういく	教育	education
れきし	歴史	history
ぶんか	文化	culture
しゃかい	社会	society
ほうりつ	法律	law
せんそう	戦争	war
へいわ	平和	peace
もくてき	目的	purpose
あんぜん	安全	safety
ろんぶん	論文	thesis, academic paper
かんけい	関係	relation, connection
ミキサー		mixer, blender
やかん		kettle
せんぬき	栓抜き	cap opener
かんきり	缶切り	can opener
かんづめ	缶詰	canned food, tinned food
ふろしき		wrapping cloth used to carry things
そろばん		abacus
たいおんけい	体温計	(clinical) thermometer

ざいりょう	材料	material, ingredient
いし	石	stone
ピラミッド		pyramid
データ		data
ファイル		file
ある 〜		a certain 〜, one 〜
いっしょうけんめい	一生懸命	with all one's effort
なぜ		why
※国連<ruby>こくれん</ruby>		United Nations
※エリーゼの ために		Für Elize
※ベートーベン		Ludwig van Beethoven, German composer (1770-1827)
※ポーランド		Poland

◁会話▷

ローン	loan
セット	set
あと	the amount left unused, the rest

····· 読み物 ·····

カップラーメン	instant Chinese noodles sold in a ready-to-use disposable container
インスタントラーメン	instant Chinese noodles
なべ	pan, pot
どんぶり	ceramic bowl
食品<ruby>しょくひん</ruby>	food
調査<ruby>ちょうさ</ruby>	investigation, survey
カップ	cup
また	and
〜の 代<ruby>か</ruby>わりに	in place of 〜, instead of 〜
どこででも	in any place
今<ruby>いま</ruby>では	now

II. Translation

Sentence Patterns

1. I am saving money in order to have my own shop in the future.
2. This pair of scissors is used to cut flowers.

Example Sentences

1. I am practicing every day in order to participate in the Bon Festival dance this summer.
   ⋯Are you? I bet you'll have a good time.
2. Why do you climb mountains alone?
   ⋯I go up mountains to be alone and meditate.
3. Are you doing anything for your health?
   ⋯No. But I think I will jog every morning from next week.
4. This is a beautiful piece.
   ⋯It's "Für Elize." It's a piece that Beethoven composed for a girl.
5. What do you use this for?
   ⋯We use it for opening wine.
6. In Japan how much money do you need to hold a wedding ceremony?
   ⋯I think you need at least 2 million yen.
   Wow, you need as much as 2 million yen?
7. Your bag is designed to contain many things, isn't it?
   ⋯Yes. As it can keep wallets, papers, handkerchiefs and other stuff separately, it is very useful for trips or work.

Conversation

What will you spend your bonus on?

Suzuki:　Ms. Hayashi, when will your bonus be paid?

Hayashi:　Next week. What about your company?

Suzuki:　Tomorrow. I'm looking forward to it. Are you?
　　　　First of all, I'll pay the loan on the car, and buy a golf set, then go on a trip....

Ogawa:　Won't you save any?

Suzuki:　Save? I've hardly thought of that.

Hayashi:　I'll save some after going on a trip to London.

Suzuki:　Are you saving money to get married?

Hayashi:　No. I think I'm going to study in Britain some day.

Ogawa:　Oh, I really envy single people. You can spend your whole bonus on yourself.
　　　　I must pay the loan on the house, and after setting aside a lot for my children's education expenses, there is hardly anything left.

III. Reference Words & Information

事務用品・道具　OFFICE SUPPLIES & TOOLS

とじる staple	はさむ・とじる clip	留める pin/tack	切る cut
ホッチキス stapler	クリップ clip	画びょう(押しピン) thumbtack	カッター　はさみ cutter　scissors

はる stick　　　　paste		削る sharpen	ファイルする file
セロテープ　ガムテープ　　のり Sellotape　packaging tape　glue		鉛筆削り pencil sharpener	ファイル file

消す erase	(穴を)あける punch	計算する calculate	(線を)引く／測る draw (a line)/measure
消しゴム　修正液 eraser　correction liquid	パンチ hole punch	電卓 calculator	定規(ものさし) ruler

切る saw	(くぎを)打つ hit (a nail)	挟む／曲げる／切る pinch/bend/cut	(ねじを)締める／緩める tighten/loosen (a screw)
のこぎり saw	金づち hammer	ペンチ pliers	ドライバー screwdriver

IV. Grammar Explanation

1.

V dictionary form	
Nの	ために、〜

in order to V
for N

This sentence pattern indicates a purpose.

① 自分の 店を 持つ ために、貯金して います。

    I am saving money in order to have my own shop.

② 引っ越しの ために、車を 借ります。   I will rent a car for the move.

③ 健康の ために、毎朝 走って います。   For my health, I jog every morning.

④ 家族の ために、うちを 建てます。   I will build a house for my family.

Nの ために is also used to mean "for the benefit of N (④)."

[Note 1] 〜ように, which you learned in Lesson 36, is also used to express a purpose. 〜ように is used with verbs that do not contain volition, while 〜ために is used with verbs that do. Compare the two sentences below.

① 自分の 店を 持つ ために、貯金して います。

⑤ 自分の 店が 持てるように、貯金して います。

    I am saving money in order to be able to have my own shop.

① means that one has intentionally set up the objective of "having a shop" and "is saving money" to attain that objective, while ⑤ means one's objective is a state in which "a shop may be gained" and one "is saving money" in order to get closer to that state.

[Note 2] なります indicates either volition (⑥) or non-volition (⑦).

⑥ 弁護士に なる ために、法律を 勉強して います。

    I study law in order to become a lawyer.

⑦ 日本語が 上手に なるように、毎日 勉強して います。

    I study everyday so that my Japanese may improve.

2.

V dictionary formの	
N	に 〜

As you learned in Lesson 38, V dictionary formの can be used as a noun phrase. V dictionary formのに and Nに are followed by such expressions as つかう、いい、べんりだ、やくに たつ、[じかんが] かかる, etc., and indicate a purpose.

⑧ この はさみは 花を 切るのに 使います。

    This pair of scissors is used to cut flowers.

⑨ この かばんは 大きくて、旅行に 便利です。

    This bag is big and convenient for trips.

⑩ 電話番号を 調べるのに 時間が かかりました。

    It took a lot of time to find the telephone number.

[Note] Different ways of expressing purpose

Let us summarize the expressions for indicating purpose that you have learned so far.

[1] V ます-form ｝に 行きます／来ます／帰ります　　　　　　　　　　　　　(L. 13)
　　N

⑪ 神戸へ 船を 見に 行きます。　　　　I'll go to Kobe to look at the ships.
⑫ 日本へ 経済の 勉強に 来ました。　　I came to Japan to study economics.

[2] V dictionary form ｝(non-volitional expression)ように、〜(volitional expression)
　　V ない-form ない　　　　　　　　　　　　　　　　　　　　　　　　(L. 36)

⑬ 早く 届くように、速達で 出します。

　　I will mail this by special delivery so that it can get there earlier.

⑭ 忘れないように、メモします。

　　I make a note so that I don't forget.

[3] V dictionary form (volitional expression) ｝ために、〜(volitional expression)
　　N の　　　　　　　　　　　　　　　　　　　　　　　　　　　　　(L. 42)

⑮ 大学に 入る ために、一生懸命 勉強します。

　　I study as hard as possible in order to enter a university.

⑯ 健康の ために、野菜を たくさん 食べます。

　　I eat a lot of vegetables for my health.

[4] V dictionary form の ｝に ｛使います／役に 立ちます／[時間が] かかります
　　N　　　　　　　　　　　｛いいです／便利です／必要です　　　　　(L. 42)

⑰ ファイルは 書類を 整理するのに 使います。

　　Files are used to put papers in order.

⑱ 近くに 店が なくて、買い物に 不便です。

　　There are no stores nearby, so it is inconvenient for shopping.

42

3.　Quantifierは

When attached to a quantifier, the particle は indicates the minimum amount that the speaker estimates is required or necessary.

⑲ 日本では 結婚式を するのに 200万円は 要ります。

　　In Japan you need at least 2 million yen to hold a wedding.

4.　Quantifierも

When attached to a quantifier, the particle も indicates that the speaker thinks that the amount mentioned is a lot.

⑳ 駅まで 行くのに 2時間も かかりました。

　　It took as long as two hours to get to the station.

㉑ うちを 建てるのに 3,000万円も 必要なんですか。

　　You need as much as 30 million yen to build a house?

105

Lesson 43

I. Vocabulary

ふえます II	増えます	[exports] increase
[ゆしゅつが～]	[輸出が～]	
へります I	減ります	[exports] decrease
[ゆしゅつが～]	[輸出が～]	
あがります I	上がります	[the price] rise
[ねだんが～]	[値段が～]	
さがります I	下がります	[the price] fall
[ねだんが～]	[値段が～]	
きれます II	切れます	[a string] break, snap
[ひもが～]		
とれます II		[a button] come off
[ボタンが～]		
おちます II	落ちます	[baggage] fall down
[にもつが～]	[荷物が～]	
なくなります I		[petrol, gasoline] run out, be lost
[ガソリンが～]		
じょうぶ[な]	丈夫[な]	strong, healthy
へん[な]	変[な]	strange, peculiar
しあわせ[な]	幸せ[な]	happy
うまい		tasty, good at
まずい		not tasty
つまらない		boring, uninteresting
ガソリン		petrol, gasoline
ひ	火	fire
だんぼう	暖房	heating
れいぼう	冷房	air-conditioning
センス		taste, sense ([ふくの] ～が あります:have good taste [in clothing])

いまにも	今にも	at any moment (used to describe a situation just before it changes)
わあ		Oh!/ Wow!

◀会 話▶

会員	member
適当[な]	suitable, proper
年齢	age
収入	income
ぴったり	exactly, just right
そのうえ	in addition to that, moreover
～と いいます	(one's name) is ～

···· 読み物 ·······

ばら	rose
ドライブ	driving

II. Translation

Sentence Patterns

1. It looks like it's about to rain any moment.
2. I'll just pop out to buy the tickets.

Example Sentences

1. The button of your jacket looks as if it's going to come off.
   ···Oh, it really is. Thank you very much.
2. It's become warmer, hasn't it?
   ···Yes. It looks as if the cherry blossoms are going to bloom soon.
3. This is German apple cake. Please try it.
   ···Oh, it looks delicious. Thank you.
4. The new section chief looks intelligent and serious, doesn't he?
   ···Yes, but he doesn't seem to have much taste in clothes.
5. There are not enough materials, are there?
   ···Would you please go and make some more photocopies?
6. I'm just going out for a while.
   ···About what time will you come back?
   I intend to be back by four.

Conversation

He looks kind

Schmidt:	What photo is that?
Watanabe:	It's an "omiai" photo.
	An "omiai" company selected it for me.
Schmidt:	Is there an "omiai" company?
Watanabe:	Yes. When you join, they put your information into a computer, as well as your preferences concerning your future partner and so on.
	Then the computer chooses a suitable partner for you.
Schmidt:	That sounds interesting.
Watanabe:	What do you think about this man?
Schmidt:	He is handsome and looks kind. A nice man!
Watanabe:	Yes. His age and income and hobbies just meet my requirements.
	Besides his surname is the same as mine, "Watanabe."
Schmidt:	Humm... Computers are amazing!

III. Reference Words & Information

性格・性質　PERSONALITY & NATURE
せいかく　せいしつ

明るい　bright　暗い　gloomy あか　　　　　　くら	活発[な]　active かっぱつ
	誠実[な]　sincere せいじつ
優しい　　　kind やさ	わがまま[な]　selfish
おとなしい　quiet, gentle	まじめ[な]　　ふまじめ[な] serious, earnest　　frivolous
冷たい　　　cold つめ	
厳しい　　　strict, severe きび	
気が長い　slow-tempered, patient き　なが	頑固[な]　stubborn がんこ
気が短い　quick-tempered き　みじか	素直[な]　obedient, gentle すなお
気が強い　　　気が弱い き　つよ　　　　き　よわ strong-willed　　timid	意地悪[な]　ill-natured, spiteful いじわる
	勝ち気[な]　competitive, unyielding か　き
	神経質[な]　nervous しんけいしつ

IV. Grammar Explanation

1. | **V ます-form**
 い-adj(〜い) ｝ そうです
 な-adj[な] | looks like

When the look of a thing leads you to a supposition, you can state your supposition using this sentence pattern. The supposition is basically based on the appearance of a thing, person, scene, etc.

1) | **V ます-form** そうです |

When the present state makes the speaker presuppose an occurrence, the speaker uses this sentence pattern to state it. いまにも, もうすぐ, これから, etc., are added to refer to the time when the speaker thinks the occurrence will take place.

① 今にも 雨が 降りそうです。

   It looks like it will rain at any moment.

② シャンプーが なくなりそうです。

   It looks like we are running out of shampoo.

③ もうすぐ 桜が 咲きそうです。

   The cherry blossoms may soon be in bloom.

④ これから 寒く なりそうです。

   It seems it'll be getting cold from now on.

2) | **い-adj(〜い)** ｝ そうです
 な-adj[な] |

This means that although something has not been confirmed as a fact, it looks so judging from the appearance.

⑤ この 料理は 辛そうです。　　　　This dish looks spicy.

⑥ 彼女は 頭が よさそうです。　　　She seems to have brains.

⑦ この 机は 丈夫そうです。　　　　This desk looks strong and durable.

[Note] When you want to describe others' feelings, adjectives expressing emotions (うれしい, かなしい, さびしい, etc.) should be used with 〜そうです. This is because you can only guess how other people feel.

⑧ ミラーさんは うれしそうです。　　Mr. Miller looks happy.

2. | **V て-form** 来ます |

1) V て-form きます means "to go somewhere, do something and come back."

⑨ ちょっと たばこを 買って 来ます。

   I'm just popping out to buy some cigarettes.

43

110

⑨ means (1) to go to the place where they sell cigarettes, (2) to buy some cigarettes there, and (3) to come back to the place where the person was.

The place where the person goes and does something is indicated by で. Exceptionally it is indicated by から when a thing is moved from the place, and the move itself is the purpose of the person's action (⑪).

⑩ スーパーで 牛乳を 買って 来ます。

I'm going to the supermarket to buy some milk (and coming back).

⑪ 台所から コップを 取って 来ます。

I'm going to fetch a glass from the kitchen.

2) N (place)へ 行って 来ます

The て-form of いきます is used before きます in this pattern, which means "to go somewhere and then come back." It is used when you don't specify the action you do at the place where you go.

⑫ 郵便局へ 行って 来ます。

I'm going to the post office (and coming back).

3) 出かけて 来ます

The て-form of でかけます is used before きます, which means "to go out and come back." It is used when you don't specify the place where you go nor the action you do at the place.

⑬ ちょっと 出かけて 来ます。　　　I'm going out (and coming back soon).

Lesson 44

I. Vocabulary

なきます I	泣きます	cry
わらいます I	笑います	laugh, smile
かわきます I	乾きます	dry
ぬれます II		get wet
すべります I	滑ります	slip
おきます II	起きます	[an accident] happen
[じこが～]	[事故が～]	
ちょうせつします III	調節します	adjust
あんぜん[な]	安全[な]	safe
ていねい[な]	丁寧[な]	polite, courteous, careful
こまかい	細かい	small, fine
こい	濃い	strong (taste), dark (color)
うすい	薄い	weak (taste), light (color)
くうき	空気	air
なみだ	涙	tear
わしょく	和食	Japanese dish
ようしょく	洋食	Western dish
おかず		side dish
りょう	量	quantity
－ばい	－倍	－ times
はんぶん	半分	half
シングル		single room
ツイン		twin-bedded room
たんす		chest of drawers
せんたくもの	洗濯物	washing, laundry
りゆう	理由	reason

◀会話▶

どう なさいますか。	What can I do for you?
カット	haircut
シャンプー	shampoo
どういうふうに なさいますか。	How would you like it done?
ショート	short
～みたいに して ください。	Do it like ～.
これで よろしいでしょうか。	Would this be all right?
［どうも］お疲れさまでした。	Thank you for being patient.

―― 読み物 ――――――――――――――――――――――――――

嫌がります Ⅰ	dislike
また	and
順序	order
表現	expression
例えば	for example
別れます Ⅱ	part, separate
これら	these things
縁起が 悪い	unlucky, ill-omened

44

II. Translation

Sentence Patterns

1. I drank too much last night.
2. This personal computer is easy to use.
3. Make this pair of trousers shorter, please.
4. Let's enjoy dancing tonight.

Example Sentences

1. Are you crying?
   ···No, I laughed so much my eyes watered.
2. Recent cars are easy to handle.
   ···Yes. But as the handling is so easy, driving is not so enjoyable for me.
3. Which is more comfortable to live in, the countryside or town?
   ···I think the countryside is more comfortable to live in.
      Because things are inexpensive, and the air is clean.
4. This glass is strong so you can't break it so easily.
   ···It is good and safe for children to use.
5. It is late at night now, so could you please be quiet?
   ···Yes. I'm sorry.
6. What shall we make tonight's dish?
   ···We ate meat yesterday. Let's make it something with fish today.
7. Let's save electricity and water, shall we?
   ···Yes, okay.
8. Chop the vegetables and stir with eggs.
   ···Yes. Is this OK?

Conversation

Do it like in this photo, please

Hairdresser: Hello. What can we do for you, today?
Lee: I'd like a haircut, please.
Hairdresser: Right then, I'll give you a shampoo, first. This way, please.

Hairdresser: How would you like your hair cut?
Lee: I'd like to have it short.
      Do it like in this photo, please.
Hairdresser: Oh, that's nice.

Hairdresser: Is this all right for the length at the front?
Lee: Let me see. Make it a little shorter, please.

Hairdresser: Here you are. How do you like it?
Lee: It's fine. Thank you.

III. Reference Words & Information

美容院・理髪店　BEAUTY PARLOR & BARBER SHOP

カット	haircut	トリートメント	treatment
パーマ	perm	ブロー	blow-dry
セット	set	ヘアダイ	hairdye
シャンプー	shampoo	そる［ひげ／顔を〜］	shave
リンス	rinse, conditioner	分ける［髪を〜］	part

耳が見えるくらいに		so that you can see my ears.
肩にかかるくらいに		to shoulder length.
まゆが隠れるくらいに	切ってください。	so that my eyebrows are covered.
１センチくらい	Please cut it	about one centimeter.
この写真みたいに		so that it looks like this photograph.

いろいろなヘアスタイル　Various Hairstyles

ボブ　bob	レイヤーカット　layered cut	ソバージュ　shaggy perm
おかっぱ　bobbed hair	三つ編み　braids	ポニーテール　ponytail
丸刈り　close-cropped cut	長髪　long hair	リーゼント　ducktail

IV. Grammar Explanation

1.
| V ます-form |
| い-adj (〜ぃ) | すぎます |
| な-adj [な] |

〜すぎます indicates that the degree of an action or a state is excessive. Therefore, it is usually used with reference to undesirable states.

① ゆうべ お酒を 飲みすぎました。   I drank too much last night.

② この セーターは 大きすぎます。   This sweater is too large (for me).

〜すぎます is classified as a Group Ⅱ verb and therefore conjugates in the same way.
    e.g., のみすぎる, のみすぎ(ない), のみすぎた

③ 最近の 車は 操作が 簡単すぎて、運転が おもしろくないです。

    The handling of recent cars is so easy that driving them is not so enjoyable for me.

④ いくら 好きでも、飲みすぎると、体に 悪いですよ。

    No matter how much you like it, drinking too much is bad for your health.

2.
| V ます-form | やすいです |
| | にくいです |

1) These phrases depict the easiness or difficulty in handling or doing something.

⑤ この パソコンは 使いやすいです。   This personal computer is easy to use.

⑥ 東京は 住みにくいです。   Living in Tokyo is difficult.

2) These phrases depict the easiness or difficulty in the characteristics of an object or a person changing or in the likelihood of something happening.

⑦ 白い シャツは 汚れやすいです。   A white shirt gets dirty easily.

⑧ 雨の 日は 洗濯物が 乾きにくいです。Things won't dry easily on a rainy day.

[Note] 〜やすい and 〜にくい function as い-adjectives and conjugate in the same way as other い-adjectives do.

⑨ この 薬は 砂糖を 入れると、飲みやすく なりますよ。

    If you add some sugar to this medicine, it will be easier to take.

⑩ この コップは 割れにくくて、安全ですよ。

    This glass won't break easily, so it is safe.

3.
```
い-adj(〜い)→〜く
な-adj[な]→に     します
N に
```

While 〜く/〜に なります that you learned in Lesson 19 indicates that something "turns into" a certain state, 〜く/〜に します, as shown in ⑪, ⑫ and ⑬, indicates that somebody "turns" something into a certain state.

⑪ 音を 大きく します。   I will turn up the volume.

⑫ 部屋を きれいに します。   I will clean my room.

⑬ 塩の 量を 半分に しました。   I reduced the amount of salt by half.

4.
```
N に します
```

N に します expresses selection and/or decision.

⑭ 部屋は シングルに しますか、ツインに しますか。

Would you like a single room or a twin room?

⑮ 会議は あしたに します。

I will set the meeting for tomorrow.

5.
```
い-adj(〜い)→〜く
な-adj[な]→に     V
```

When changing adjectives into the forms written above, they function as adverbs.

⑯ 野菜を 細かく 切って ください。

Please cut the vegetables into small pieces.

⑰ 電気や 水は 大切に 使いましょう。

Let's conserve electricity and water.

Lesson 45

I.　Vocabulary

あやまります Ⅰ	謝ります	apologize
あいます Ⅰ		encounter [an accident]
[じこに～]	[事故に～]	
しんじます Ⅱ	信じます	believe, trust
よういします Ⅲ	用意します	prepare
キャンセルします Ⅲ		cancel
うまく いきます Ⅰ		go well
ほしょうしょ	保証書	guarantee
りょうしゅうしょ	領収書	receipt
おくりもの	贈り物	gift, present (～を します: give a present)
まちがいでんわ	まちがい電話	wrong (telephone) number
キャンプ		camp
かかり	係	person in charge
ちゅうし	中止	calling off, cancelling, suspension
てん	点	point, score
レバー		lever
[－えん]さつ	[－円]札	[－yen] note, bill
ちゃんと		regularly, properly
きゅうに	急に	suddenly

たのしみに して います	楽しみに して います	be looking forward to, be expecting
いじょうです。	以上です。	That's all.

◁会話▷

係員	person in charge, attendant
コース	course
スタート	start
－位	-th (ranking)
優勝します Ⅲ	win the championship

····· 読み物 ···

悩み	trouble, worry
目覚まし[時計]	alarm clock
眠ります Ⅰ	sleep
目が 覚めます Ⅱ	wake up
大学生	university student
回答	answer, reply
鳴ります Ⅰ	ring
セットします Ⅲ	set
それでも	nevertheless, for all that

45

II. Translation

Sentence Patterns

1. In the event that you lose your credit card, please inform the credit card company at once.
2. She did not come, even though she promised.

Example Sentences

1. What should I say for an apology when I dial a wrong number?
   ⋯You should say, "I'm sorry, I have a wrong number."
2. This is the guarantee for this computer.
   If something goes wrong, contact this number, please.
   ⋯I see.
3. Excuse me, but can I get a receipt for photocopy charges in this library?
   ⋯Yes, you can. Please tell the clerk when you need one.
4. In case of fire or earthquake, do not use the elevator.
   ⋯Yes.
5. Did you make a good speech?
   ⋯No. I forgot the words in the middle, though I knew it by heart after a lot of practice.
6. Are you going to play golf in spite of this rain?
   ⋯Yes. I like it very much, though I am not good at it.

Conversation

Though I practiced very hard

Attendant: Everybody, this marathon race is for your health. So don't overdo it, please. If you feel sick, please tell an attendant near you.

Participants: OK.

Attendant: In case you go the wrong way, go back to the last point on the correct route and resume running.

Participant: Excuse me. If I want to quit, what should I do?

Attendant: In that case, please give your name to the nearest attendant and leave. Now it's time to start.

Suzuki: Mr. Miller, how was the marathon race?

Miller: I got the second prize.

Suzuki: The second? That's great!

Miller: Oh, no. Considering I practiced as hard as I could, it's disappointing that I couldn't win.

Suzuki: You will have another chance next year.

III. Reference Words & Information

非常の場合　EMERGENCY

〔1〕地震の場合　In Case of Earthquake

1）備えが大切　Prepare first.

① 家具が倒れないようにしておく

Be sure to fix furniture so that it will not fall over.

② 消火器を備える・水を貯えておく

Have a fire extinguisher on hand.

Keep an emergency supply of water.

③ 非常用持ち出し袋を用意しておく

Keep items needed in an emergency in a bag.

④ 地域の避難場所を確認しておく

Make sure you know where the evacuation point is in your district.

⑤ 家族、知人、友人と、もしもの場合の連絡先を決めておく

Decide on a contact address with your family, friends and acquaintances.

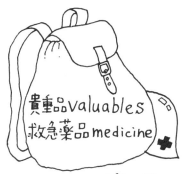

2）万一地震が起きた場合　When an Earthquake Strikes

① すばやく火の始末

Immediately extinguish any fire in use.

② 戸を開けて出口の確保

Open doors to secure an exit path.

③ 慌てて外に飛び出さない

Do not panic or rush outside.

④ テーブルの下にもぐる

Get under a table.

3）地震が収まったら　When an Earthquake Stops

正しい情報を聞く（山崩れ、崖崩れ、津波に注意）

Get accurate information.

(Beware of landslides and tidal waves.)

4）避難する場合は　When You Evacuate

車を使わず、必ず歩いて

Do not evacuate by car, but walk.

〔2〕台風の場合　In Case of Typhoon

① 気象情報を聞く　　Listen to the weather forecast.

② 家の周りの点検　　Check the exterior of the house.

③ ラジオの電池の備えを Have radio batteries on hand.

④ 水、緊急食品の準備 Keep a supply of water and food.

121

IV. Grammar Explanation

1.

V dictionary form	
V た-form	
V ない-formない	
い-adj (～い)	場合は、～
な-adjな	
Nの	

～ばあいは is an expression used to talk about a hypothetical situation. The sentence after it indicates how to cope with such a situation or its consequence. ばあいは follows either verbs, adjectives or nouns. Because ばあい is a noun, the forms of verbs, い-adjectives, な-adjectives and nouns connected to it are the same as the forms when modifying nouns.

① 会議に 間に 合わない 場合は、連絡して ください。

   If you cannot be in time for the meeting, please inform us.

② 時間に 遅れた 場合は、会場に 入れません。

   If you are late, you will not be admitted to the hall.

③ ファクスの 調子が 悪い 場合は、どう したら いいですか。

   In the event that the fax machine does not work well, what should I do?

④ 領収書が 必要な 場合は、係に 言って ください。

   When you need a receipt, please tell the person in charge.

⑤ 火事や 地震の 場合は、エレベーターを 使わないで ください。

   In case of fire or earthquake, do not use the elevator.

2.

V	plain form	
い-adj	plain form	のに、～
な-adj	plain form	
N	～だ→～な	

のに follows either verbs, adjectives or nouns. Their forms used with のに are as shown above. のに is used when what is stated in the second clause runs contrary to what is expected from the first clause.

⑥ 約束を したのに、彼女は 来ませんでした。

   She did not come, even though she promised.

⑦ きょうは 日曜日なのに、働かなければ なりません。

   Even though today is Sunday, I have to work.

In ⑥, the speaker expects that the woman will come because she promised to do so. So he naturally feels disappointed that she did not come. In ⑦, Sunday is normally a holiday, yet the speaker has to work so he feels dissatisfied. The second clause implies feelings of unexpectedness or dissatisfaction.

45

[Note] The difference between 〜のに and 〜が／〜ても:

⑧ わたしの 部屋は 狭いですが、きれいです。　　　　　　　（×狭いのに）

My room is small but clean.

⑨ あした 雨が 降っても、出かけます。　　　　　　　　　（×雨が 降るのに）

Even if it rains tomorrow, I will go out.

〜が and 〜ても in ⑧ and ⑨ cannot be substituted with 〜のに. This is because ⑧ simply joins two different evaluations together and the second clause therein does not represent an unexpected consequence of what is stated in the first clause. The first clause of ⑨ suggests a possibility, but 〜のに can only indicate things that have actually occurred in reality.

⑩ 約束を したのに、どうして 来なかったんですか。　（×約束を しましたが）

You promised to come. Why didn't you come?　　　　　　　（×約束を しても）

〜のに in ⑩ cannot be substituted with 〜が or 〜ても. This is because the second clause expresses a strong reproach.

Lesson 46

I. Vocabulary

やきます Ⅰ	焼きます	bake, grill, roast
わたします Ⅰ	渡します	hand over
かえって きます Ⅲ	帰って 来ます	come back
でます Ⅱ ［バスが～］	出ます	[a bus] leave, depart
るす	留守	absence
たくはいびん	宅配便	delivery service
げんいん	原因	cause
ちゅうしゃ	注射	injection
しょくよく	食欲	appetite
パンフレット		pamphlet
ステレオ		stereo
こちら		my place, my side
～の ところ	～の 所	the place around ～
ちょうど		just, exactly
たったいま	たった今	just now (used with the past tense; indicates completion)

いま いいでしょうか。 今 いいでしょうか。   May I bother you now?

ガスサービスセンター	gas service center
ガスレンジ	gas range, gas cooker
具合 ぐあい	condition
どちら様でしょうか。 さま	Who is this, please?
向かいます Ⅰ む	head for
お待たせしました。 ま	Sorry to have kept you waiting.

······ 読み物 ···

知識 ちしき	knowledge
宝庫 ほうこ	treasury
手に 入ります ［情報が～］ Ⅰ て はい じょうほう	[information] come in, reach
システム	system
例えば たと	for example
キーワード	key word
一部分 いちぶぶん	one part
入力します Ⅲ にゅうりょく	input
秒 びょう	second
出ます ［本が～］ Ⅱ で ほん	[a book] be published

II. Translation

Sentence Patterns

1. The conference is just about to begin.
2. He just graduated from university this March.
3. I sent the documents by special delivery, so they should arrive tomorrow.

Example Sentences

1. Hello, this is Tanaka speaking. Can you talk now?
   ···I'm afraid I am going out just now.
   I will call you when I get back.
2. Have you found the cause of the breakdown?
   ···No, we are checking now.
3. Is Ms. Watanabe in?
   ···Well, she has just left now.
   She might be still at the elevator.
4. How are you getting along with your work?
   ···I joined the company just last month, so I can't say yet.
5. I only bought this video camera last week, and already it doesn't work.
   ···Well, let me see it.
6. Will Teresa's temperature go down?
   ···I've given her a shot now, so it should go down within three hours.

Conversation

He should be there soon

Man at Gas Service Center:	Hello, Gas Service Center.
Thawaphon:	Er, there's a problem with my gas stove.
Man:	What seems to be the trouble?
Thawaphon:	Well, although you only fixed it last week, the flame goes out right away. It's dangerous, so could you come and fix it soon?
Man:	I see. We'll be there around five. May I have your name and address?

Thawaphon:	Hello. A man was supposed to be coming here around five o'clock to check my gas stove. Isn't he coming?
Man:	I'm sorry. Who is this, please?
Thawaphon:	My name is Thawaphon.
Man:	Hold a moment. I'll contact our repairman.

Man:	Sorry to have kept you waiting. He is heading for your place now. He'll be there in about 10 minutes.

III. Reference Words & Information

かたかな語のルーツ　ROOTS OF KATAKANA WORDS

Japanese has many loanwords from foreign languages. They are written in katakana. While most katakana words come from English, some of them have come from French, Dutch, German, Portuguese, etc. Katakana words are also created by the Japanese using foreign words.

	食べ物・飲み物 food & drink	衣服 clothes	病気 illness	芸術 arts	その他 others
英語	ジャム　ハム jam　　ham クッキー cookie チーズ cheese	エプロン apron スカート skirt スーツ suit	インフルエンザ influenza ストレス stress	ドラマ drama コーラス chorus メロディー melody	スケジュール schedule ティッシュペーパー tissues トラブル　レジャー trouble　leisure
フランス語	コロッケ croquette オムレツ omelette ピーマン green pepper	ズボン trousers ランジェリー lingerie キュロット culotte		バレエ ballet シャンソン chanson アトリエ studio	アンケート questionnaire コンクール competition ピエロ pierrot, clown
ドイツ語	フランクフルト [ソーセージ] frankfurter		レントゲン X-ray ノイローゼ neurosis アレルギー allergy	メルヘン fairy tale	アルバイト part-time job エネルギー energy ゲレンデ　テーマ ski slope　theme
オランダ語	ビール beer コーヒー coffee	ズック deck shoes ホック hook	メス scalpel ピンセット tweezers		ゴム　　ペンキ rubber　paint ガラス　コック glass　　cook
ポルトガル語	パン bread カステラ sponge cake	ビロード velvet チョッキ vest, waistcoat			カルタ card
イタリア語	マカロニ macaroni スパゲッティ spaghetti			オペラ opera バレリーナ ballerina	

IV. Grammar Explanation

1.
V dictionary form	
V て-form いる	ところです
V た-form	

The word ところ originally means "place," but it is also used to indicate a temporal position. The ところ that you learn in this lesson is the latter and is used to stress a certain point in time during the course of an action.

1) | V dictionary form ところです |

This sentence pattern shows that a person is about to start doing something or something is about to start. It may be used together with これから, [ちょうど] いまから, etc., which makes the meaning clearer.

① 昼ごはんは もう 食べましたか。

　…いいえ、これから 食べる ところです。

Have you had lunch yet?

　…No, I'm going to have it now.

② 会議は もう 始まりましたか。

　…いいえ、今から 始まる ところです。

Has the meeting begun yet?

　…No, it's just beginning now.

2) | V て-form いる ところです |

This sentence pattern shows that a person is now doing a certain action or a certain action is now being done. It is often used with いま.

③ 故障の 原因が わかりましたか。

　…いいえ、今 調べて いる ところです。

Do you know what caused the breakdown?

　…No. We are investigating it now.

3) | V た-form ところです |

This sentence pattern shows that a person has just finished a certain action or a certain action has just been completed. It is used together with たったいま, etc.

④ 渡辺さんは いますか。

　…あ、たった今 帰った ところです。

　まだ エレベーターの 所に いるかも しれません。

Is Ms. Watanabe here?

　…Oh, she's just left.

　She may be somewhere near the elevator.

⑤ たった今 バスが 出た ところです。

The bus left just now.

[Note] 〜ところです is a noun sentence and is used in various structures. See ⑥ below.

⑥ もしもし 田中ですが、今 いいでしょうか。

…すみません。今から 出かける ところなんです。

Hello. This is Tanaka speaking. May I talk to you now?

…Sorry. I'm just going out.

2. | V た-form ばかりです |

This sentence pattern means that not much time has passed since a certain action or event occurred. It is the expression of the speaker's feeling and can be used regardless of the real length of time that has passed if the speaker feels it is short. In this respect, this sentence pattern is different from V た-form ところです, which can only indicate the time when a certain action has just been completed.

⑦ さっき 昼ごはんを 食べた ばかりです。

I had lunch only a while ago.

⑧ 木村さんは 先月 この 会社に 入った ばかりです。

Ms. Kimura joined this company only a month ago.

[Note] 〜ばかりです is a noun sentence and is used in various structures. See ⑨ below.

⑨ この ビデオは 先週 買った ばかりなのに、調子が おかしいです。

I bought this video only a week ago, but it isn't working well.

3. | V dictionary form
V ない-form ない
い-adj(〜い)
な-adjな
N の | はずです |

The speaker uses this sentence pattern to show he/she is convinced of what is stated before はずです. By using this sentence pattern, the speaker implies that he/she has grounds to think so, that it is his/her own judgement, and that he/she is quite sure of it.

⑩ ミラーさんは きょう 来るでしょうか。

…来る はずですよ。きのう 電話が ありましたから。

Do you think Mr. Miller will come today?

…I'm sure he'll come. I received a phone call from him yesterday.

In ⑩, the grounds for the speaker's judgement is yesterday's phone call. Based on this call, the speaker himself judges that Mr. Miller will come today. The speaker shows his/her firm belief in this judgement by using 〜 はずです.

Lesson 47

I. Vocabulary

あつまります I ［ひとが〜］	集まります ［人が〜］	[people] gather
わかれます II ［ひとが〜］	別れます ［人が〜］	[people] part, separate
ながいきします III	長生きします	live long
します III ［おと/こえが〜］ ［あじが〜］ ［においが〜］	［音/声が〜］ ［味が〜］	[sound/ voice] be heard taste smell
さします I ［かさを〜］	［傘を〜］	put up [an umbrella]
ひどい		terrible, severe
こわい	怖い	frightening, horrible
てんきよほう	天気予報	weather forecast
はっぴょう	発表	announcement, presentation
じっけん	実験	experiment
じんこう	人口	population
におい		smell
かがく	科学	science
いがく	医学	medicine, medical science
ぶんがく	文学	literature
パトカー		patrol car
きゅうきゅうしゃ	救急車	ambulance
さんせい	賛成	approval, agreement
はんたい	反対	objection, opposition
だんせい	男性	male, man
じょせい	女性	female, woman

どうも	it appears that (used when making a tentative judgement)
～に よると	according to ～ (indicates the source of information)
※バリ[島]	Bali [island] (in Indonesia)
※イラン	Iran
※カリフォルニア	California (in U. S. A.)
※グアム	Guam

◁会 話▷

恋人	sweetheart, boyfriend, girlfriend
婚約します Ⅲ	get engaged
相手	the other person
知り合います Ⅰ	get acquainted

······ 読み物 ···

平均寿命	average life span
比べます［男性と～］ Ⅱ	compare [with men]
博士	doctor
脳	brain
ホルモン	hormone
化粧品	cosmetics
調べ	survey, research
化粧	makeup (～を します: put on makeup)

II. Translation

Sentence Patterns

1. According to the weather forecast, it's getting colder tomorrow.
2. Someone seems to be in the next room.

Example Sentences

1. The newspaper says that a Japanese speech competition will be held in January. Why don't you enter it, Mr. Miller?
    ···Well, I'll think about it.
2. I heard that Klara lived in France in her childhood.
    ···That's why she can understand French, too.
3. They say that Power Electric's new electronic dictionary is very good because it's easy-to-use.
    ···Yes, it is. I've already bought it.
4. I went to the Indonesian island of Bali recently.
    ···I hear that it is a very beautiful place.
    Yes. It was very wonderful.
5. They're lively, aren't they?
    ···Yes. It seems that they are having a party or something.
6. There are a lot of people gathered.
    ···It looks as if there's been an accident. There's a police car and an ambulance.

Conversation

I heard that she has got engaged

Watanabe: I'm going now. Good-bye.
Takahashi: Ms. Watanabe, just a moment. I'll come with you.
Watanabe: I'm sorry but I'm in a hurry.

Takahashi: Ms. Watanabe leaves earlier recently.
            It looks like she has found a boyfriend.
Hayashi: Oh, don't you know the news? They say that she got engaged recently.
Takahashi: Really? Who? The lucky man!
Hayashi: Mr. Suzuki of IMC.
Takahashi: Mr. Suzuki?
Hayashi: I heard that she met him last year at the wedding reception of one of her friends.
Takahashi: Did she?
Hayashi: By the way, how about you, Mr. Takahashi?
Takahashi: Me? My work is my sweetheart.

III. Reference Words & Information

擬音語・擬態語　ONOMATOPOEIA

ザーザー（降る） (rain) hard	ピューピュー（吹く） (wind be) whistling	ゴロゴロ（鳴る） (thunder) loudly
ワンワン（ほえる） bowwow	ニャーニャー（鳴く） meow	カーカー（鳴く） caw
げらげら（笑う） guffaw	しくしく（泣く） sob	きょろきょろ（見る） (look around) restlessly
ぱくぱく（食べる） (eat) heartily	ぐうぐう（寝る） (be) fast asleep	すらすら（読む） (read) fluently
ざらざら（している） (feel) rough	べたべた（している） (be) sticky	つるつる（している） (be) smooth, slippery

IV. Grammar Explanation

1. | plain form そうです | I hear that ...

This is an expression for conveying information you have obtained from another source without adding your own point of view. When the source of the information is given, it is indicated by 〜に よると (according to〜), placed at the beginning of the sentence.

① 天気予報に よると、あしたは 寒く なるそうです。

According to the weather forecast, it will be cold tomorrow.

② クララさんは 子どもの とき、フランスに 住んで いたそうです。

I heard that Klara lived in France when she was a child.

③ バリ島は とても きれいだそうです。

I hear that Bali is very beautiful.

[Note 1] Note that this expression is different in meaning and construction from 〜そうです used for describing an apparent state that you learned in Lesson 43. Compare the following sentences.

④ 雨が 降りそうです。　　　　　　It looks like rain.　　　　　　(L. 43)

⑤ 雨が 降るそうです。　　　　　　I heard that it will rain.

⑥ この 料理は おいしそうです。　This food looks delicious.　　(L. 43)

⑦ この 料理は おいしいそうです。I heard that this food is delicious.

[Note 2] The difference between 〜そうです (expression of hearsay) and 〜と いって いました (L. 33):

⑧ ミラーさんは あした 京都へ 行くそうです。

I hear that Mr. Miller is going to Kyoto tomorrow.

⑨ ミラーさんは あした 京都へ 行くと 言って いました。

Mr. Miller said that he is going to Kyoto tomorrow.

In example ⑨ the information source is Mr. Miller himself, while in example ⑧ it is highly possible that the information source is not necessarily Mr. Miller but somebody else. Another difference is that in example ⑨ the words which Mr. Miller said can be quoted directly or indirectly. In example ⑧ on the other hand, only the plain form may be used.

47

134

2.

V	plain form
い-adj	plain form
な-adj	plain form～*だ*→～*な*
N	plain form～*だ*→～*の*

$\left.\right\}$ようです   It seems that ...

～ようです conveys the speaker's subjective conjecture, which is based on the information obtained through his/her sensory organs.

A sentence that ends in ようです sometimes accompanies どうも which suggests the speaker cannot be certain if what he/she is saying is a fact.

⑩ 人が 大勢 集まって いますね。

…事故のようですね。パトカーと 救急車が 来て いますよ。

Look, there is a big crowd.

…It looks like there's been an accident. A patrol car and an ambulance are there.

⑪ せきも 出るし、頭も 痛い。どうも かぜを ひいたようだ。

I have a cough and a headache. It looks like I've caught a cold.

[Note] The difference between ～そうです (L. 43, describing an apparent state) and ～ようです:

⑫ ミラーさんは 忙しそうです。   Mr. Miller seems to be busy.   (L. 43)

⑬ ミラーさんは 忙しいようです。   It seems that Mr. Miller is busy.

Example ⑫ indicates an intuitive judgement based on what the speaker has seen of Mr. Miller's condition or behavior, and example ⑬ indicates the speaker's judgement based on what he has read, heard or been told.

3. 声／音／におい／味が します

⑭ 変な 音が しますね。   There's a strange sound, isn't there?

A phenomenon that is perceivable by the senses is described by using ～が します. Expressions in this category are こえが します, においが します, and あじが します. All these expressions mean that these things have been perceived or sensed regardless of the speaker's intention.

Lesson 48

I.　Vocabulary

おろします Ⅰ	降ろします、下ろします	put down, lower
とどけます Ⅱ	届けます	deliver, report
せわを します Ⅲ	世話を します	take care of 〜
いや［な］	嫌［な］	unwilling, reluctant
きびしい	厳しい	strict, hard
じゅく	塾	cram school
スケジュール		schedule
せいと	生徒	pupil
もの	者	person (referring to one's relatives or subordinates)
にゅうかん	入管	Immigration Bureau
さいにゅうこくビザ	再入国ビザ	re-entry visa
じゆうに	自由に	freely
〜かん	〜間	for 〜 (referring to duration)
いい ことですね。		That's good.

◁会話▷

お忙しいですか。 (いそが)	Are you busy? (used when talking to someone senior or older)
久しぶり (ひさ)	after a long time
営業 (えいぎょう)	business, sales
それまでに	by that time
かまいません。	It's all right./It doesn't matter.
楽しみます I (たの)	enjoy oneself

····· 読み物 ·······

もともと	originally
−世紀 (せいき)	-th century
代わりを します III (か)	be a substitute, be a replacement
スピード	speed
競走します III (きょうそう)	race
サーカス	circus
芸 (げい)	performance, trick
美しい (うつく)	beautiful
姿 (すがた)	figure, appearance
心 (こころ)	heart, mind
とらえます II	catch
〜に とって	for 〜

II. Translation

Sentence Patterns

1. I will send my son to Britain to study.
2. I will make/let my daughter learn the piano.

Example Sentences

1. When you arrive at the station, please call me.
    I will send a member of my staff to the station to pick you up.
    ···All right.
2. Your Hans likes to play outside, doesn't he?
    ···Yes. Playing outside is good for his health, and gives him a chance to make friends, so I encourage him to play in the open air.
3. Hello, can I speak to Ichiro, please?
    ···I'm sorry. He is in the bath at the moment.
    I will tell him to call you back later.
4. How is Professor Watt's class?
    ···It's very strict. He never allows the students to use Japanese.
    But he lets them freely say what they want to say.
5. Excuse me. Could you let me park the car here for a while? I'm unloading packages.
    ···All right.

Conversation

Let me take leave, please

Miller: Ms. Nakamura, are you busy now?

Nakamura: No, go ahead.

Miller: I've got something to ask you.

Nakamura: What is it?

Miller: Well. A friend of mine in America is going to marry next month.

Nakamura: Uh-huh.

Miller: So I would like to be allowed to return to my country.

Nakamura: When next month?

Miller: Could you let me have 10 days leave or so from the 7th?
As I haven't seen my parents for a long time either.

Nakamura: Well, we are to have the sales meeting on the 20th, right?
Can you return before that?

Miller: The wedding is to be held on the 15th, so I'll come back soon after it's over.

Nakamura: Then, it's OK. Have a good time and refresh yourself.

Miller: Thank you.

III.　Reference Words & Information

しつける・鍛^{きた}える　DISCIPLINE

子^こどもに何^{なに}をさせますか　What will you make or let your children do?

● 自然^{しぜん}の中^{なか}で遊^{あそ}ぶ
  play outdoors in natural surroundings

● スポーツをする
  do sports

● 一人^{ひとり}で旅行^{りょこう}する
  go on a trip alone

● いろいろな経験^{けいけん}をする
  have various experiences

● いい本^{ほん}をたくさん読^よむ
  read many good books

● お年寄^{としよ}りの話^{はなし}を聞^きく
  listen to old people

● ボランティアに参加^{さんか}する
  participate in voluntary activities

● うちの仕事^{しごと}を手伝^{てつだ}う
  do some household chores

● 弟^{おとうと}や妹^{いもうと}、おじいちゃん、おばあちゃんの世話^{せわ}をする
  take care of their sister, brother, grandfather and grandmother

● 自分^{じぶん}がやりたいことをやる
  do what they want to do

● 自分^{じぶん}のことは自分^{じぶん}で決^きめる
  make decisions by themselves

● 自信^{じしん}を持^もつ
  have confidence

● 責任^{せきにん}を持^もつ
  take responsibility

● 我慢^{がまん}する
  be patient

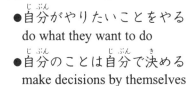

● 塾^{じゅく}へ行^いく
  go to 'juku (cram school)'

● ピアノや英語^{えいご}を習^{なら}う
  learn to play the piano, English and so on

IV. Grammar Explanation

1. Causative verbs

How to make causative verbs (See Main Textbook, Lesson 48, p. 188, 練習A1.)

		Causative verbs	
		polite form	plain form
I	いきます	いかせます	いかせる
II	たべます	たべさせます	たべさせる
III	きます	こさせます	こさせる
	します	させます	させる

All causative verbs are Group II verbs; they conjugate into the dictionary form, ない-form, て-form, etc.

e.g. いかせる, いかせ (ない), いかせて

2. Causative verb sentences

There are two types of causative sentences: those which indicate the subject of an action with を, and those which indicate it with に. When the verb is intransitive, as in 1) below, を is used, while when the verb is transitive, as in 2), に is used irrespective of whether the object of the verb is stated or not.

1) | N (person)を V (intransitive) causative |　make/let a person V (intransitive verb)

① 部長は 加藤さんを 大阪へ 出張させます。

The department manager makes Mr. Kato go to Osaka on business.

② わたしは 娘を 自由に 遊ばせました。

I let my daughter play freely.

[Note] When an intransitive verb with "N (place)を" is used in the sentence, the subject of the action is indicated with に, as shown in ③, but without a phrase with を, the subject of the action is indicated with を, as shown in ④.

③ わたしは 子どもに 道の 右側を 歩かせます。

I make my child walk on the right side of the road.

④ わたしは 子どもを 歩かせます。　I make my child walk.

2) | N (person)に N を V (transitive) causative |　make/let a person V (transitive verb)

⑤ 朝は 忙しいですから、娘に 朝ごはんの 準備を 手伝わせます。

I am busy in the morning, so I make my daughter help prepare breakfast.

⑥ 先生は 生徒に 自由に 意見を 言わせました。

The teacher let her students freely voice their opinions.

3. Usage of a causative

Causative verbs indicate compulsion or permission. A causative sentence is used when the relationship between a senior person and a junior person is very clear (e.g., a parent and child, an elder brother and younger brother, a superior and subordinate, etc.) and the senior person forces the junior person to do a certain act, or allows him to do something. ① and ⑤ are examples of compulsion and ② and ⑥ are those of permission. But when the speaker tells a person from outside his own group that he will make someone from within his group do something, as seen in the example below, the causative sentence is used regardless of their status.

⑦ 駅に 着いたら、お電話を ください。
　係の 者を 迎えに 行かせますから。

　…わかりました。

When you arrive at the station, please call me.

I will send a member of my staff to the station to pick you up.

…Thank you.

[Note 1] When a junior person has a senior person do a certain action and the senior versus junior relationship between them is obvious, Ｖ て-form いただきます is used. If the two are equal or the relationship is delicate in terms of which one is senior, Ｖ て-form もらいます is used instead.

⑧ わたしは 部長に 説明して いただきました。

I had the department manager explain it to me.

⑨ わたしは 友達に 説明して もらいました。

I had my friend explain it to me.

[Note 2] As shown in ⑧ above, a causative verb usually cannot be used to describe a junior person having a senior person do something. However, as can be seen in ⑩, there is an exception when verbs denoting emotion such as あんしんする, しんぱいする, がっかりする, よろこぶ (be glad), かなしむ (feel sad), おこる(get angry), etc., are used. The Main Textbook, however, does not cover this usage.

⑩ 子どもの とき、体が 弱くて、母を 心配させました。

When I was a child, my poor health worried my mother.

4. | **Ｖ causative て-form いただけませんか** | Would you please let me do ...?

In Lesson 26 you learned Ｖ て-form いただけませんか, which is used to request someone to do something. Ｖ causative て-form いただけませんか, on the other hand, is used to seek permission.

⑪ コピー機の 使い方を 教えて いただけませんか。

Would you please tell me how to use the photocopier?　　　　　　　　　　(L. 26)

⑫ 友達の 結婚式が あるので、早退させて いただけませんか。

As I'm going to attend my friend's wedding, would you please let me leave earlier?

(L. 48)

In ⑪ おしえる will be done by the listener, while in ⑫ そうたいする will be done by the speaker.

Lesson 49

I. Vocabulary

つとめます II 　[かいしゃに～]	勤めます 　[会社に～]	work [for a company]
やすみます I	休みます	go to bed, sleep
かけます II 　[いすに～]	掛けます	sit on [a chair]
すごします I	過ごします	spend (time), pass (time)
よります I 　[ぎんこうに～]	寄ります 　[銀行に～]	drop into [a bank]
いらっしゃいます I		be, go, come (respectful equivalent of います, いきます and きます)
めしあがります I	召し上がります	eat, drink (respectful equivalent of たべます and のみます)
おっしゃいます I		say (respectful equivalent of いいます)
なさいます I		do (respectful equivalent of します)
ごらんに なります I	ご覧に なります	see, look at (respectful equivalent of みます)
ごぞんじです	ご存じです	know (respectful equivalent of しって います)
あいさつ		greeting, address (～を します : greet, give an address)
はいざら	灰皿	ashtray
りょかん	旅館	Japanese-style hotel or inn
かいじょう	会場	meeting place, hall
バスてい	バス停	bus stop
ぼうえき	貿易	trade
～さま	～様	(respectful equivalent of ～さん)
かえりに	帰りに	on the way back
たまに		once in a while
ちっとも		not at all (used with negatives)
えんりょなく	遠慮なく	without reserve, without hesitation

－年－組	class －of -th grade
では	well, then (polite equivalent of じゃ)
出します ［熱を～］ I	run [a fever]
よろしく お伝え ください。	Give my best regards./Please say hello.
失礼いたします。	Good-bye. (humble equivalent of しつれいします)
※ひまわり小学校	fictitious elementary school

······ 読み物 ···

講師	lecturer
多くの ～	many ～, much ～
作品	work (of art, etc.)
受賞します Ⅲ	be awarded a prize
世界的に	world-wide
作家	novelist, writer
～で いらっしゃいます I	be (respectful equivalent of です)
長男	one's eldest son
障害	handicap, defect
お持ちです	have (respectful way of saying もって います)
作曲	composition (music)
活動	activity
それでは	well, so (indicating an end or beginning)
※大江 健三郎	Japanese novelist (1935-)
※東京大学	Tokyo University
※ノーベル文学賞	Nobel Prize for literature

49

II. Translation

Sentence Patterns

1. The section chief has already gone home.
2. The company president has already gone home.
3. The department manager will go to America on business.
4. Please wait a moment.

Example Sentences

1. Have you read all of this book?
   ···Yes, I have read it all.
2. Excuse me. Are you going to use that ashtray?
   ···No, I'm not. Please use it.
3. Do you often go to the movies?
   ···No, I don't. But, I watch a movie on TV occasionally.
4. Do you know that Mr. Ogawa's son has passed the entrance exam for Sakura University?
   ···No, I didn't know at all until now.
5. What would you like to drink?
   Please feel free to ask for anything you like.
   ···I'll have a beer, please.
6. Is Manager Matsumoto there?
   ···Yes, he is in this room. Please go in.

Conversation

Would you please convey my message?

Teacher: Hello, this is Himawari elementary school.

Klara: Good morning.
This is Mrs. Schmidt speaking. I'm the mother of Hans Schmidt, a pupil in Class Two of the fifth grade. May I speak to Ms. Ito?

Teacher: She's not here yet.

Klara: Then, would you please pass a message to her?

Teacher: Yes, certainly. What is it?

Klara: Hans ran a fever last night and he still has it this morning.

Teacher: Oh, that's bad.

Klara: So, I'm making him stay at home today. Could you tell that to Ms. Ito, please?

Teacher: I see. I hope he gets better soon.

Klara: Thank you. Good-bye.

III. Reference Words & Information

電話のかけ方　TALKING ON THE TELEPHONE

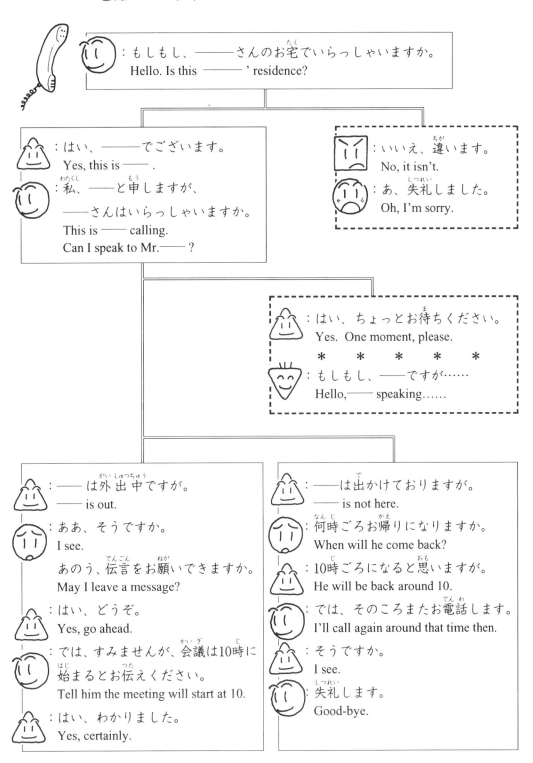

: もしもし、————さんのお宅でいらっしゃいますか。
Hello. Is this ———— ' residence?

: はい、————でございます。
Yes, this is ——— .

: 私、———と申しますが、
————さんはいらっしゃいますか。
This is ——— calling.
Can I speak to Mr.———?

: いいえ、違います。
No, it isn't.

: あ、失礼しました。
Oh, I'm sorry.

: はい、ちょっとお待ちください。
Yes. One moment, please.
*　*　*　*　*
: もしもし、———ですが……
Hello,——— speaking……

: ———は外出中ですが。
——— is out.

: ああ、そうですか。
I see.
あのう、伝言をお願いできますか。
May I leave a message?

: はい、どうぞ。
Yes, go ahead.

: では、すみませんが、会議は10時に
始まるとお伝えください。
Tell him the meeting will start at 10.

: はい、わかりました。
Yes, certainly.

: ———は出かけておりますが。
——— is not here.

: 何時ごろお帰りになりますか。
When will he come back?

: 10時ごろになると思いますが。
He will be back around 10.

: では、そのころまたお電話します。
I'll call again around that time then.

: そうですか。
I see.

: 失礼します。
Good-bye.

49

145

IV. Grammar Explanation

1. 敬語(けいご) (honorific expressions)

You learn けいご in Lesson 49 and 50. けいご are expressions used to show the speaker's respect for the listener or the person being referred to. The speaker is expected to show respect depending on his/her relationship with the listener or the person being referred to. There are the following three factors that should be considered in deciding the use of けいご: (1) When the speaker is junior or lower in social status, he/she uses けいご to show respect to the person senior or higher in social status. (2) When the speaker does not have a close acquaintanceship with the listener, as is typical when the speaker first meets the listener, he/she uses けいご to show respect to the listener. (3) The ウチ-ソト relationship should also be taken into consideration with regard to the use of けいご. The speaker's group such as his/her family and company, etc., are considered as ウチ, and other groups are considered as ソト. When the speaker talks about ウチの ひと (an insider) to ソトの ひと (an outsider), the insider is treated like the speaker himself/herself. Therefore, even if the insider is senior or higher in status, the speaker cannot use けいご in the way that shows respect to the insider.

2. Types of 敬語(けいご)

けいご are classified into three types: そんけいご (respectful expressions), けんじょうご (humble expressions) and ていねいご (polite expressions). Lesson 49 deals with そんけいご.

3. 尊敬語(そんけいご) (respectful expressions)

そんけいご are expressions used to describe the listener or the person referred to, as well as things connected with him/her and his/her actions.

1) Verbs

(1) **Respectful verbs** (See Main Textbook, Lesson 49, p. 196, 練習(れんしゅう)A1.)

The same verbs used in the passive are used as respectful verbs. They are Group II verbs.

① 中村(なかむら)さんは 7時(じ)に 来(こ)られます。　　　Mr. Nakamura is coming at seven.

② お酒(さけ)を やめられたんですか。　　　Have you given up drinking?

(2) | お V ます-form に なります |

This pattern is considered politer than the respectful verbs mentioned above. Verbs whose ます-form consist of one mora (みます, ねます, etc.) and Group III verbs cannot be used in this pattern. As for the verbs which have special equivalents (see (3) below), note that the special equivalents rather than this pattern are used.

③ 社長(しゃちょう)は もう お帰(かえ)りに なりました。　　　The president has already left for home.

(3) **Special respectful words** (See Main Textbook, Lesson 49, p. 196, 練習(れんしゅう)A5.)

Some verbs have special respectful equivalents. They are considered to show the same level of respect as (2) above.

④ ワット先生(せんせい)は 研究室(けんきゅうしつ)に いらっしゃいます。　Professor Watt is in the office.

⑤ どうぞ 召(め)し上(あ)がって ください。　　　Please help yourselves.

[Note] いらっしゃいます, なさいます, くださいます and おっしゃいます are Group Ⅰ verbs, but except for the ます-form, they change their form in the ら-row when they conjugate.

⑥ ワット先生は テニスを なさいますか。　　Does Professor Watt play tennis?

　　…いいえ、なさらないと 思います。　　…No, I don't think so.

(4) おVます-form ください

This is the respectful way of instructing or inviting someone to do something.

⑦ あちらから お入り ください。　　Please enter from over there.

[Note] The special words you learned in (3) above cannot be used in this pattern. The exceptions are めしあがります and ごらんに なります, which are changed to おめしあがり ください (Please help yourself) and ごらん ください (Please have a look at it) respectively.

2) Nouns, adjectives and adverbs

In addition to verbs, some nouns, adjectives and adverbs can be turned into そんけいご by attaching お or ご to the front of the word. The choice between お and ご depends on the word. Basically お is attached to words of Japanese origin, while ご is attached to words of Chinese origin.

Examples of words to which お is attached:

(N)　　お国、お名前、お仕事

(な-adj) お元気、お上手、お暇

(い-adj) お忙しい、お若い

Examples of words to which ご is attached:

(N)　　ご家族、ご意見、ご旅行

(な-adj) ご熱心、ご親切

(adverb) ご自由に

49

147

4. 敬語 and style of sentence

A sentence can end with a plain form of けいご, which makes the sentence a plain style sentence. This kind of sentence appears on occasions such as when the speaker is talking with a close friend about a person to whom the speaker wishes to show respect.

⑧ 部長は 何時に いらっしゃる？　　What time will the general manager come?

5. Uniform level of 敬語 in a sentence

In honorific expressions, replacing some of the words in a sentence with けいご does not suffice. It is necessary to keep a uniform level of けいご throughout the entire sentence.

⑨ 部長の 奥様も ごいっしょに ゴルフに 行かれます。

The general manager's wife will go golfing together with him.

In ⑨, おくさま and ごいっしょに are used instead of おくさん and いっしょに in order to be consistent with the respectful verb いかれます.

6. ～まして

You change Vて-form to Vます-form まして when you want to be very polite. In a sentence with けいご, ～まして is often used for consistency.

⑩ ハンスが ゆうべ 熱を 出しまして、けさも まだ 下がらないんです。

Hans became feverish last night and still has a fever this morning.

Lesson 50

I.   Vocabulary

まいります I	参ります	go, come (humble equivalent of いきます and きます)
おります I		be (humble equivalent of います)
いただきます I		eat, drink, receive (humble equivalent of たべます, のみます and もらいます)
もうします I	申します	say (humble equivalent of いいます)
いたします I		do (humble equivalent of します)
はいけんします Ⅲ	拝見します	see (humble equivalent of みます)
ぞんじます Ⅱ	存じます	know (humble equivalent of しります)
うかがいます I	伺います	ask, hear, visit (humble equivalent of ききます and いきます)
おめに かかります I	お目に かかります	meet (humble equivalent of あいます)
ございます I		be (polite equivalent of あります)
～で ございます		be (polite equivalent of ～です)
わたくし	私	I (humble equivalent of わたし)
ガイド		guide
おたく	お宅	(someone else's) house
こうがい	郊外	suburbs
アルバム		album
さらいしゅう	さ来週	the week after next
さらいげつ	さ来月	the month after next
さらいねん	さ来年	the year after next
はんとし	半年	half a year
さいしょに	最初に	first of all
さいごに	最後に	lastly
ただいま	ただ今	now

※江戸東京博物館　　　　　Edo-Tokyo Museum

◁会話▷

緊張します Ⅲ	become tense, be strained
放送します Ⅲ	broadcast
撮ります［ビデオに〜］Ⅰ	record [on video], video
賞金	prize money
自然	nature
きりん	giraffe
象	elephant
ころ	times, days
かないます［夢が〜］Ⅰ	[dream] be realized
ひとこと よろしいでしょうか。	May I say one word?
協力します Ⅲ	cooperate
心から	from my heart
感謝します Ⅲ	be grateful, be thankful

······ 読み物 ······

［お］礼	gratitude, thanks
拝啓	Dear 〜
美しい	beautiful
お元気で いらっしゃいますか。	How are you doing? (respectful equivalent of おげんきですか)
迷惑を かけます Ⅱ	trouble, annoy, inconvenience
生かします Ⅰ	make good use of
［お］城	castle
敬具	Sincerely yours
※ミュンヘン	Munich (in Germany)

II. Translation

Sentence Patterns

1. I will send this month's schedule.
2. I come from America.

Example Sentences

1. It looks heavy. Shall I help you hold it?
   ···Oh, yes, please.
2. Excuse me, where are we visiting after seeing this place?
   ···We are taking you to the Edo-Tokyo Museum.
3. Mr. Gupta is arriving at two o'clock, isn't he? Is somebody going to pick him up?
   ···Yes, I will go.
4. Where does your family live?
   ···My family lives in New York.
5. May I see your ticket, please?
   ···Sure.
   Thank you very much.
6. Do you know that Mr. Miller won the first prize at the speech contest?
   ···Yes, I heard it from the department manager.
7. This is Mr. Miller.
   ···How do you do? My name is Miller.
   I am pleased to meet you.
8. Is there a telephone near here?
   ···Yes, it's next to the staircase over there.

Conversation

I am sincerely grateful to you

Master of Ceremonies:	Congratulations on winning the championship. It was a wonderful speech.
Miller:	Thank you very much.
M.C.:	Did you feel tense?
Miller:	Yes, I felt very tense.
M.C.:	Did you know that this would be broadcast on TV?
Miller:	Yes. I want to video it and let my parents in America see it.
M.C.:	What will you spend the prize money on?
Miller:	Let me see. I like animals, and I've had a dream of going to Africa since my childhood.
M.C.:	Then you'll go to Africa?
Miller:	Yes. I think I would like to see giraffes and elephants in the wild.
M.C.:	It means the dream you have had since childhood will come true.
Miller:	Yes. Er, may I say something?
M.C.:	Please.
Miller:	I would like to express my sincerest thanks to all the people for their cooperation and help so that I could participate in this speech contest.

III. Reference Words & Information

封筒・はがきのあて名の書き方　HOW TO WRITE ADDRESSES

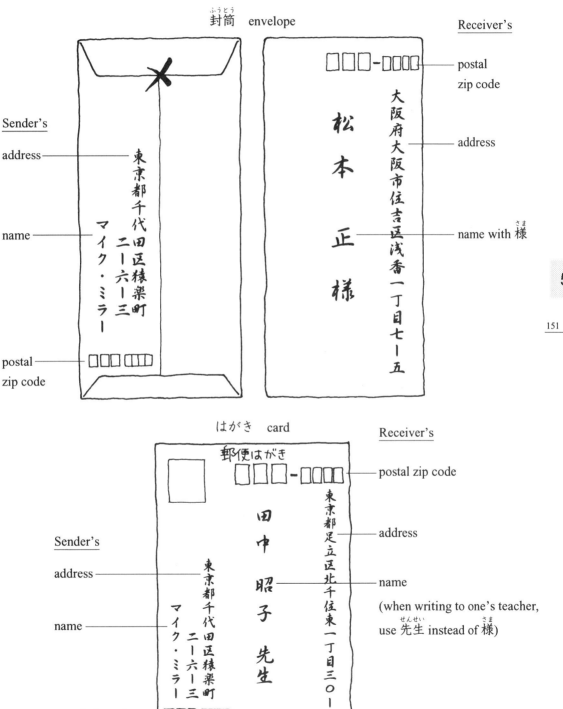

封筒　envelope

Receiver's
postal zip code
address
name with 様

Sender's
address
name
postal zip code

はがき　card

Receiver's
postal zip code
address
name
(when writing to one's teacher, use 先生 instead of 様)

Sender's
address
name
postal zip code

IV. Grammar Explanation

1. 謙譲語 (humble expressions)

けんじょうご are expressions in which the speaker humbles himself/herself and lowers his/her own acts to show respect to the listener or the person being referred to. Respect is directed at a person of higher social status or ソトの ひと (an outsider). けんじょうご is also used when the speaker refers to ウチの ひと (an insider) in front of an outsider.

1) | お／ご〜します |

(1) | お V (I , II group)ます-form します |

① 重そうですね。お持ちしましょうか。

It looks so heavy. Shall I carry it for you?

② 私が 社長に スケジュールを お知らせします。

I will tell the president the schedule.

③ 兄が 車で お送りします。

My elder brother will take you in his car.

In examples ① and ②, the speaker humbles himself/herself by lowering his/her acts to show his/her respect to the listener (①) or the person being referred to (②). In example ③, the action is performed by an insider, not by the speaker.

This form is not applicable to verbs in which the ます-form consists of one mora as in みます or います.

(2) | ご V (III group) |

④ 江戸東京博物館へ ご案内します。

I will take you to the Edo-Tokyo Museum.

⑤ きょうの 予定を ご説明します。

I will explain today's schedule.

This pattern is applicable to Group III verbs. Other than those verbs given in the examples above, only those verbs which imply some association with the listener such as しょうかいします, しょうたいします, そうだんします and れんらくします can be used. でんわします and やくそくします are exceptions in that お instead of ご precedes them.

[Note] The patterns in (1) and (2) can only be used with acts which involve another person beside the agent of the act. Therefore, they are not applicable to an act that does not involve another person such as the one in the following example.

× 私は 来月 国へ お帰りします。

2) Special humble verbs (See Main Textbook, Lesson 50, p. 204, 練習 A3.)

There are some verbs which contain humble meanings. They are used as follows.

(1)When the speaker's act involves the listener or the person to whom respect is directed:

⑥ 社長の 奥様に お目に かかりました。

I met the president's wife.

⑦ あしたは だれが 手伝いに 来て くれますか。

…私が 伺います。

Who will come over to help me tomorrow?

…I will.

(2)When the speaker's act does not involve the listener or the person to whom respect is directed:

⑧ ミラーと 申します。　　　　My name is Miller.

⑨ アメリカから 参りました。　I come from the United States.

2. 丁寧語 (polite expressions)

ていねいご are polite expressions used to show the speaker's respect to the listener.

1) ございます

ございます is the polite equivalent of あります.

⑩ 電話は 階段の 横に ございます。

The pay phone is beside the stairs.

2) ～で ございます

～で ございます is the polite equivalent of です.

⑪ はい、IMCで ございます。

…パワー電気の シュミットですが、 ミラーさん、 お願いします。

Hello, this is IMC.

…This is Schmidt of Power Electric. May I speak to Mr. Miller?

3) よろしいでしょうか

よろしいでしょうか is a polite equivalent of いいですか.

⑫ お飲み物は 何が よろしいでしょうか。

…コーヒーを お願いします。

What would you like to drink?

…Coffee, please.

⑬ この パンフレットを いただいても よろしいでしょうか。

May I have one of these pamphlets?

Particles

1. [は]

    A: 1) I don't like sports.   (Lesson 26)

        2) In my school, there is an American teacher. (27)

        3) This vending machine is broken. (29)

    B: 1) In the old days we could see mountains well from here, but not now. (27)

        2) I can write hiragana, but not kanji. (27)

        3) On a fine day, you can see Mt. Fuji, but not on a rainy day. (27)

    C: You need at least ten people for preparing a party. (42)

2. [も]

    A: 1) There is an American teacher in my brother's school, too. (27)

        2) I have a fever and a headache, so I will take a day off work. (28)

    B: It took as long as three weeks to have the video fixed. (42)

3. [の]

    A: 1) The trip is scheduled to be for one week. (31)

        2) Please assemble the table according to the directions. (34)

        3) I'll have coffee after eating. (34)

        4) I eat a lot of vegetables for my health. (42)

        5) When it breaks down, please phone this number. (45)

        6) That supermarket should be closed tomorrow. (46)

        7) What Mr. Ogawa said seems to be true. (47)

        8) Mr. Gupta is arriving at two o'clock. (50)

    B: It is a small town in Hokkaido where my daughter was born. (38)

4. [を]

    A: I will graduate from university. (31)

    B: I don't make phone calls after eleven at night. (36)

    C: The department manager let Mr. Suzuki take three days off work. (48)

5. [が]

    A: 1) The bus didn't come. (26)

        2) We can see mountains from the window. (27)

        3) A big bridge has been completed nearby. (27)

        4) The light is on. (29)

        5) There is a picture hung on the wall. (30)

        6) I will do it, so please leave it as it is. (30)

        7) A new star has been discovered. (37)

        8) People in Tokyo walk fast. (38)

        9) I didn't understand it because the explanation was difficult. (39)

10) I will go and meet Mr. Gupta. (50)

B: I can read Japanese newspapers. (27)

C: I want to tour NHK. How can I do that? (26)

6. [に]

A: 1) I was late for the appointment. (26)

   2) I'm going to participate in the athletic meeting. (26)

   3) I passed the entrance examination to Sakura University. (32)

   4) I noticed that I had left something behind. (34)

   5) I am going to take part in a baseball game tomorrow. (36)

   6) I met with an accident. (45)

   7) I'll work for a company. (49)

B: 1) You can see an island over there. (35)

   2) I left my umbrella in a train. (29)

   3) There is a picture hung on the wall. (30)

C: 1) That teacher is popular with the students. (28)

   2) I am interested in computers. (41)

D: 1) I go to university by car. (28)

   2) I'm thinking of going to a hot spring resort with my family. (31)

   3) I will be transferred to Fukuoka next month. (31)

E: 1) Let's ask Ms. Watanabe to unlock the door. (29)

   2) Could you please tell the section chief that tomorrow is inconvenient for me? (33)

F: I was asked to do something by the department manager. (37)

G: Do you know that Ms. Kimura had a baby? (38)

H: The department manager gave me this plate for a wedding gift. (41)

I: This bag is light and useful for trips. (42)

J: The next meeting is to be held in two weeks time. (44)

K: I will make/let my daughter learn the piano. (48)

7. [で]

A: 1) You can reach the station in 30 minutes. (32)

   2) If you don't have any opinions, let's close this meeting now. (35)

   3) Will this length do for the trousers? (44)

B: 1) Would you please speak a little bit louder? (27)

   2) You had better not carry it in cash. (32)

C: This dress is made of paper. (37)

D: Because of the earthquake a lot of people died. (39)

8. [と]

   1) I'm thinking of establishing my own company in the future. (31)

   2) "Stop" is written over there. (33)

3) This kanji reads "Kin'en." (33)

4) Please tell Mr. Suzuki that I will wait for him in the meeting room. (33)

9. ［から］

Sake is made from rice. (37)

10. ［か］

1) Men go to weddings dressed in a black or a dark blue suit. (34)

2) They can't tell yet whether or not typhoon number 9 will come to Tokyo. (40)

3) Please check what time JL107 will arrive. (40)

11. ［しか］

I can only take a week off at my company. (27)

12. ［とか］

Everyday I take exercise such as dancing, swimming, and the like. (36)

How to Use the Forms

1. [ます-form]

ます-formながら ～	I listen to music while eating.　　(Lesson 28)
ます-formやすいです	This personal computer is easy to use.　　(44)
ます-formにくいです	This glass is strong so you can't break it so easily.　　(44)
おます-formに なります	The company president has already gone home.　　(49)
おます-form ください	Please wait a moment.　　(49)
おます-formします	I will send this month's schedule.　　(50)

2. [て-form]

て-form います	I jog every morning.　　(28)
	The window is closed.　　(29)
て-form いません	I haven't written my report yet.　　(31)
て-form しまいます	I left my umbrella in a train.　　(29)
て-form あります	There is a map of the town affixed to the wall in the police box.　　(30)
て-form おきます	I will prepare before lessons.　　(30)
て-form みます	I try putting on new shoes.　　(40)
て-form いただきます	My teacher corrected the errors in my letter.　(41)
て-form くださいます	My department chief's wife taught me the tea ceremony.　　(41)
て-form やります	I made a paper airplane for my son.　　(41)
て-form いただけませんか	Could you kindly introduce a good teacher to me?　　(26)
て-form きます	I'll just pop out to buy the tickets.　　(43)

3. [ない-form]

ない-formないで、～	I walk to the station instead of taking a bus.(34)
ない-formなく なります	Because the sea has become dirty, we can no longer swim here.　　(36)

4. [dictionary form]

dictionary form な	Don't make noise in the train. (33)
dictionary form ように なります	I've finally become able to ride a bicycle. (36)
dictionary form のは　〜	Drawing pictures is fun. (38)
dictionary form のが　〜	I like looking at the stars. (38)
dictionary form のを　〜	I forgot to bring my wallet. (38)
dictionary form　ために、〜	I am saving money in order to have my own shop. (42)
dictionary form のに　〜	This pair of scissors is used to cut flowers. (42)

5. [た-form]

た-form あとで、〜	I brush my teeth after eating. (34)
た-form ばかりです	I joined the company just last month. (46)

6. [volitional form]

volitional form と おもって います	I'm thinking of establishing my own company in the future. (31)

7.

dictionary form ない-form ない ｝つもりです	I intend to buy a car next month. (31) I don't intend to go home this year. (31)
dictionary form ない-form ない ｝ように、〜	I send the letter by special delivery so that it arrives earlier. (36) I write down phone numbers so I don't forget them. (36)
dictionary form ない-form ない ｝ように します	I try to write in my diary every day. (36) Please be sure you're not late. (36)

8.

dictionary form て-form いる ｝ところです た-form	The game is just about to start. (46) I'm checking the cause now. (46) The bus has just gone. (46)

9.

た-form ない-form ない ｝ほうが いいです	You had better take exercise every day. (32) You had better not take a bath today. (32)

10.

て-form ない-form ないで ｝〜	I'll go out with my umbrella. (34) I sent a letter without a stamp. (34)

11. [plain form]

plain form し、〜	Subways are fast and inexpensive, so let's take the subway. (28)
plain form と いって いました	Mr. Miller said that he would go on a business trip to Osaka next week. (33)
plain form そうです	According to the weather forecast, it will get colder tomorrow. (47)

verb plain form のを ～			Do you know that they have built a big hotel in front of the station? (38)

verb			It will snow tomorrow. (32)
い-adjective	plain form	でしょう	It will be cold tomorrow. (32)
な-adjective	plain form		The stars will be beautiful tonight. (32)
noun	～だ		It will be fine tomorrow. (32)

verb			He may resign from his company. (32)
い-adjective	plain form	かも しれません	He may be busy tomorrow. (32)
な-adjective	plain form		He may be free next week. (32)
noun	～だ		He may be ill. (32)

verb			I don't know when the meeting will end. (40)
い-adjective	plain form	か、 ～	Please think what is good for a present. (40)
な-adjective	plain form		I'll make sure where the emergency exit is. (40)
noun	～だ		

verb			Please let me know whether or not you can attend the year-end party. (40)
い-adjective	plain form	か どうか、 ～	I'll phone to ask whether or not it is convenient. (40)
な-adjective	plain form		I don't know whether the story is true or not. (40)
noun	～だ		

verb			Why were you late? (26)
い-adjective	plain form	んです	I felt bad. (26)
な-adjective	plain form		The air conditioner is out of order. (26)
noun	～だ→～な		

verb			I have something to do, so I'll leave now. (39)
い-adjective	plain form	ので、 ～	I'm going to go to bed early tonight because I have a headache. (39)
な-adjective	plain form		I bought a bottle of wine because today is my birthday. (39)
noun	～だ→～な		

verb			She did not come, even though she promised. (45)
い-adjective	plain form	のに、 ～	Even though the work is busy, the salary is low. (45)
な-adjective	plain form		My husband doesn't cook for me so often, though he is good at cooking. (45)
noun	～だ→～な		

verb 〉plain form い-adjective 〉 な-adjective plain form noun 〜だ→〜な	のは 〜	It was last March that I came to Japan. (38) It is Seiji Ozawa's concert CD that I want to get. (38) It is the health of my family that is most important. (38)

verb 〉plain form い-adjective 〉 な-adjective plain form 〜だ→〜な noun plain form 〜だ→〜の	ようです	Someone seems to be in the next room. (47) It seems that my department manager doesn't like golf. (47) It looks as if there's been an accident. (47)

12. verb ます-form
い-adjective (〜ン) 〉そうです
な-adjective [な]

It looks like it's about to rain any moment. (43)
This cake looks delicious. (43)
That man looks serious. (43)

verb ます-form
い-adjective (〜ン) 〉すぎます
な-adjective [な]

I drank too much last night. (44)
This question is too difficult. (44)
This method is too complicated. (44)

13. verb 〈 て-form
ない-form なくて 〉
い-adjective 〜くて 〉、〜
な-adjective で
noun で

I was surprised to hear the news. (39)
I miss my family. (39)
I can't go on Saturday because it's not convenient. (39)
The story is complicated, so I don't understand it well. (39)

14. verb dictionary form 〉
noun の 〉よていです

The airplane is due to arrive at nine o'clock. (31)
The meeting is scheduled for Wednesday. (31)

15. verb 〈 dictionary form
た-form 〉 とおりに、〜
noun の

Please write down exactly what I say from now. (34)
Tell me about it as you saw it, please. (34)
Please push the button according to the number. (34)

16. verb 〈 dictionary form
た-form
ない-form ない 〉
い-adjective 〉 ばあいは、〜
な-adjective な
noun の

In the event that you lose your credit card, please inform the credit card company at once. (45)
If the photocopier goes wrong, contact this number, please. (45)
Please tell us when you need a receipt. (45)

17. verb 〈 dictionary form
ない-form ない 〉
い-adjective 〉 はずです
な-adjective な
noun の

The parcel should arrive tomorrow. (46)
The section chief is supposed to be good at German. (46)
The supermarket should be closed tomorrow. (46)

Various Uses of Verbs and Adjectives

1. たかい (い-adjective)→たかく (adverb)

はやい	I am going home early since it is my child's birthday today. (Lesson 9)	
はやい	I practice swimming every day so that I can swim fast.	(36)
くわしい	I will explain how to operate (the machine) in detail.	(44)
おおきい	Please write the letters bigger.	(44)

2. げんき [な] (な-adjective)→げんきに (adverb)

じょうず[な]	I want to be able to make green tea well.	(36)
たいせつ[な]	Let's conserve water.	(44)
きれい[な]	Please tidy up the desk.	(44)
ていねい[な]	You had better speak to the manager more politely.	(44)
かんたん[な]	I will briefly explain the schedule .	(44)

3. おおきい (い-adjective)　→おおきく なります。
げんき [な] (な-adjective)→げんきに なります。
かしゅ(noun)　　　　→かしゅに なります。

あつい	From now on, it will get hotter and hotter.	(19)
じょうず[な]	You have become good at Japanese.	(19)
いしゃ	I want to be a doctor.	(19)
10じ	Let's leave at 10 o'clock.	(25)

4. おおきい (い-adjective)　→おおきく します。
きれい[な] (な-adjective)→きれいに します。
はんぶん (noun)　　　　→はんぶんに します。

みじかい	I will make my trousers a little shorter.	(44)
ちいさい	Please make this figure smaller.	(44)
しずか[な]	As it is late, would you please be quiet?	(44)
2ばい	I will double the amount of water.	(44)
ショート	I want my hair cut short.	(44)

5. おおきい (い-adjective)→おおきさ(noun)

ながい	The length of that bridge is 3,911 meters.	(40)
たかい	I will measure my height.	(40)
おもい	What is the weight of this package?	(40)

6. やすみます(verb)→やすみ (noun)

おわります	I will climb Mt. Fuji at the end of August.	(20)
はなします	The teacher's talk yesterday was interesting.	(21)
かえります	Please drop in at my house on your way home.	(49)
たのしみます	I am looking forward to the trip in the summer vacation.	(35)
もうしこみます	You must apply for the speech contest by tomorrow.	(40)

7. はな(noun)を みます(verb)→[お]はなみ (noun)

やまに のぼります	I would like to go mountain climbing. Don't you know any good place?	(35)
かんを きります	A can opener is used for opening cans.	(42)

8. かきます(verb)→かきかた (noun)

よみます	Please tell me how to read this kanji.	(14)
つかいます	Please teach me how to use chopsticks.	(16)
はいります	Mr. Yamada explained to me how to take a Japanese-style bath.	(24)
します	I will explain how to operate a videotape recorder.	(44)

Intransitive and Transitive Verbs

transitive / intransitive	L.	て-form	Examples
きります	7	きって	Please cut the sheet of paper.
きれます	43	きれて	The string seems to be breaking.
あけます	14	あけて	I open the door.
あきます	29	あいて	The door opens.
しめます	14	しめて	Please shut the door.
しまります	29	しまって	The door is closed.
つけます	14	つけて	I turned on the light.
つきます	29	ついて	The light does not come on.
けします	14	けして	Please turn off the light.
きえます	29	きえて	The light is off.
とめます	14	とめて	May I park my car here?
とまります	29	とまって	A car is parked in front of my house.
はじめます	14	はじめて	Let's begin the meeting.
はじまります	31	はじまって	Has the meeting begun yet?
うります	15	うって	They sell magazines at the supermarket.
うれます	28	うれて	This magazine sells well.
いれます	16	いれて	Please put the beer in the refrigerator.
はいります	13	はいって	There's beer in the refrigerator.
だします	16	だして	I take the ticket out of my pocket.
でます	23	でて	Push this button, and the ticket will come out.
なくします	17	なくして	I've lost my key.
なくなります	43	なくなって	The key is lost.
あつめます	18	あつめて	I collected many stamps.
あつまります	47	あつまって	Many stamps are gathered together.
なおします	20	なおして	I'll have my bicycle repaired.
なおります	32	なおって	I have recovered from my illness.
かえます	23	かえて	I'll change the time for the party.
かわります	35	かわって	The time for the party has changed.
きを つけます	23	きを つけて	I'll be careful in order that there's no mistake.
きが つきます	34	きが ついて	I noticed a mistake later.

transitive / intransitive	L.	て -form	Examples
おとします	29	おとして	I've lost my wallet.
おちます	43	おちて	There's a wallet on the ground.
とどけます	29	とどけて	I'll take the papers to the manager.
とどきます	36	とどいて	The papers have arrived.
ならべます	30	ならべて	I put the chairs in rows.
ならびます	39	ならんで	People are standing in a line.
かたづけます	30	かたづけて	I put the parcels in order.
かたづきます	26	かたづいて	The parcels have been put in order.
もどします	30	もどして	I put the pair of scissors back in the drawer.
もどります	33	もどって	The manager will come back soon.
みつけます	31	みつけて	It's hard to find a job.
みつかります	34	みつかって	A job is difficult to find.
つづけます	31	つづけて	We'll continue the meeting.
つづきます	32	つづいて	The meeting is still in session.
あげます	33	あげて	If you understand, please raise your hand.
あがります	43	あがって	The fever goes up.
さげます	33	さげて	I'll lower the price to sell.
さがります	43	さがって	The price has fallen.
おります	34	おって	It's me that broke the branch.
おれます	29	おれて	The branch is broken.
こわします	37	こわして	The child has broken the clock.
こわれます	29	こわれて	That clock is broken.
よごします	37	よごして	The child made the clothes dirty.
よごれます	29	よごれて	The clothes are dirty.
おこします	37	おこして	I wake up my child.
おきます	4	おきて	My child gets up at seven.
かけます	38	かけて	I lock the door.
かかります	29	かかって	The door is locked.
やきます	46	やいて	I bake bread.
やけます	39	やけて	The bread is done.

Adverbs and Adverbial Expressions

1. さっき   You had a phone call from home a while ago.   (Lesson 34)

    たったいま   I got up just now.   (46)

    いつか   I want to build a house for myself some day.   (27)

    このごろ   Ms. Watanabe leaves for home early these days.   (36)

    しばらく   When sleepy, I park my car and sleep a while.   (28)

    ずっと   I intend to live in Japan for a long time.   (31)

    いつでも   You can tour NHK at any time.   (26)

    たいてい   I mainly draw pictures on my days off.   (28)

    たまに   I don't go to the movies often, but watch old ones on TV occasionally.   (49)

2. さきに   You eat something sweet before drinking the tea.   (34)

    さいしょに   First let me introduce Mr.Tanaka.   (50)

    さいごに   The last one that goes out of the room should turn off the light, please.   (50)

3. きちんと   The books are tidily put in rows.   (38)

    ちゃんと   Although I take medicine as instructed, I can't get rid of my cold.   (45)

    ぴったり   This pair of shoes fits my feet perfectly.   (43)

    はっきり   I can't hear you clearly. Please talk in a louder voice.   (27)

    いっしょうけんめい   I'll work hard in order to own a shop.   (42)

    じゆうに   The teacher let the students give their opinions freely.   (48)

    ちょくせつ   I heard this story directly from my teacher.   (26)

    きゅうに   I heard that he cannot come because he has suddenly got something to do.   (45)

4. ずいぶん   They are having a good time, aren't they?   (26)

    かなり   I can understand the news on TV fairly well.   (36)

    もっと   Keep it in mind to eat more vegetables.   (36)

    できるだけ   I make it a rule not to eat sweet thing as much as possible.   (36)

    ちっとも   I didn't know at all that Mr. Ogawa's son had passed the entrance exam to Sakura University.   (49)

    ほとんど   I've read most of the books he wrote.   (27)

    I could hardly do yesterday's exam.   (27)

    あんなに   As he has been studying that hard, he is sure to pass the exam.   (32)

165

5. かならず   When you are absent from the company, always be sure to inform us beforehand.   (36)

ぜったいに   Make sure never to be late.   (36)

たしか   His birthday is, let me see, February 15th if I remember correctly.   (29)

もしかしたら   I'm afraid I might not be able to graduate in March.   (32)

いまにも   It looks like it will begin raining at any moment.   (43)

ちょうど   The game is just about to start.   (46)

どうも   It seems there was an accident.   (47)

まだ   The meeting room is still in use.   (30)

もう   It's all up. I can't run any further.   (33)

やっと   I've finally become able to ride a bicycle.   (36)

Various Conjunctions

1. ～ながら   I will show photographs while I explain it.   (Lesson 28)

     ～し   The price is reasonable, and the taste is good, too, so, I always eat at this restaurant.   (28)

     それに   Professor Watt is earnest, studious, and moreover has a lot of experience.   (28)

     そのうえ   His age, income and hobbies just fit what I want to a T. In addition to that, his name is the same as mine, too.   (43)

2. それで   Here the stores are nice and there is somewhere to eat...

         …So, it's crowded with people.   (28)

     ～て   I was surprised to hear the news.   (39)

     ～くて   Saturday is not convenient for me, so I can't come.   (39)

     ～で   I could not understand that movie well because the story was complicated.   (39)

         The bus was delayed by an accident.   (39)

     ～ので   I have something to do, so please excuse me.   (39)

         Today is my birthday, so I bought a bottle of wine.   (39)

3. ～のに   Though she promised to come, she didn't.   (45)

         Even though it's a holiday, I have to work.   (45)

4. ～ば   When the spring comes, cherry blossoms bloom.   (35)

         If it's fine, you can see an island over there.   (35)

     ～なら   If you want to go to a hot spring resort, I recommend Hakuba.   (35)

     ～ばあいは   When you take a day off work, please inform us by phone.   (45)

         When you lose a ticket, please tell a station employee.   (45)

         When you need a receipt, please contact us.   (45)

5. では   Well, it's time that I went.   (45)

6. ところで   Hans got a good grade.

         …Did he? I'm glad to hear that.

         By the way, it will soon be sports day. Will your husband come, too?   (40)

Contributors

田中よね　*Yone Tanaka*
The Association for Overseas Technical Scholarship
Matsushita Electric Industrial Co., LTD. Overseas Training Center
Coordinator of Japanese Language Course

牧野昭子　*Akiko Makino*
The Association for Overseas Technical Scholarship
The Japan Foundation Japanese-Language Institute, Kansai

重川明美　*Akemi Shigekawa*
The Association for Overseas Technical Scholarship
Matsushita Electric Industrial Co., LTD. Overseas Training Center

御子神慶子　*Keiko Mikogami*
The Association for Overseas Technical Scholarship
Matsushita Electric Industrial Co., LTD. Overseas Training Center

古賀千世子　*Chiseko Koga*
Kobe University International Students Center
Matsushita Electric Industrial Co., LTD. Overseas Training Center

沢田幸子　*Sachiko Sawada*
Osaka YWCA College Japanese Language Department
The Center for Student Exchange, Kyoto University

新矢麻紀子　*Makiko Shinya*
Osaka University International Student Center
Matsushita Electric Industrial Co., LTD. Overseas Training Center

Editorial Advisors

石沢弘子　*Hiroko Ishizawa*
The Association for Overseas Technical Scholarship

豊田宗周　*Munechika Toyoda*
The Association for Overseas Technical Scholarship

Illustrators

佐藤夏枝　*Natsue Sato*
向井直子　*Naoko Mukai*

みんなの日本語　初級II
翻訳・文法解説　英語版

1998年7月10日　初版第1刷発行
2006年3月3日　第10刷発行

編著者　株式会社　スリーエーネットワーク
発行者　高井道博
発　行　株式会社　スリーエーネットワーク
〒101-0064 東京都千代田区猿楽町2-6-3 （松栄ビル）
電話　　営業 03(3292)5751
　　　　編集 03(3292)6521
http://www.3anet.co.jp

印　刷　日本印刷株式会社

不許複製　　　　　　　　ISBN4-88319-108-7 C0081
落丁・乱丁本はお取替えいたします。

初級日本語教材の定番 みんなの日本語シリーズ

みんなの日本語初級Ⅰ

本冊	2,625円	漢字英語版	1,890円
本冊・ローマ字版	2,625円	漢字カードブック	630円
翻訳・文法解説ローマ字版（英語）	2,100円	初級で読めるトピック25	1,470円
翻訳・文法解説英語版	2,100円	書いて覚える文型練習帳	1,365円
翻訳・文法解説中国語版	2,100円	漢字練習帳	945円
翻訳・文法解説韓国語版	2,100円	聴解タスク25	2,100円
翻訳・文法解説スペイン語版	2,100円	教え方の手引き	2,940円
翻訳・文法解説フランス語版	2,100円	練習C・会話イラストシート	2,100円
翻訳・文法解説ポルトガル語版	2,100円	導入・練習イラスト集	2,310円
翻訳・文法解説タイ語版	2,100円	カセットテープ	6,300円
翻訳・文法解説インドネシア語版	2,100円	CD	5,250円
翻訳・文法解説ロシア語版	2,100円	携帯用絵教材	6,300円
翻訳・文法解説ドイツ語版	2,100円	B4サイズ絵教材	37,800円
標準問題集	945円	会話ビデオ	10,500円

みんなの日本語初級Ⅱ

本冊	2,625円	漢字英語版	1,890円
翻訳・文法解説英語版	2,100円	初級で読めるトピック25	1,470円
翻訳・文法解説中国語版	2,100円	書いて覚える文型練習帳	1,365円
翻訳・文法解説韓国語版	2,100円	漢字練習帳	1,260円
翻訳・文法解説スペイン語版	2,100円	教え方の手引き	2,940円
翻訳・文法解説フランス語版	2,100円	練習C・会話イラストシート	2,100円
翻訳・文法解説ポルトガル語版	2,100円	導入・練習イラスト集	2,520円
翻訳・文法解説タイ語版	2,100円	カセットテープ	6,300円
翻訳・文法解説インドネシア語版	2,100円	CD	5,250円
翻訳・文法解説ロシア語版	2,100円	携帯用絵教材	6,825円
翻訳・文法解説ドイツ語版	2,100円	B4サイズ絵教材	39,900円
標準問題集	945円	会話ビデオ	10,500円

みんなの日本語初級　やさしい作文　1,260円

ホームページで
新刊や日本語セミナーを
ご案内しております
http://www.3anet.co.jp

価格は税込です　スリーエーネットワーク